The Medium Within

By John Rogers

Acknowledgment

There are a lot of players in the writing of this book so it becomes difficult to place all them here in a short paragraph and make it sound worthy of their support.

I must start off with Patricia Quinn, my shadow, who has always been beside me in my efforts of either my work as an author or my work as a Medium.

Dr. Steven Rudin a true close friend who has taken a great deal of his time to critique my work with the eyes of an eagle making sure that I get my message across in the right manner.

George Kipp, one that says little but does a masterful job as he sets to work at a computer and produces masterpieces that become the envy of all who see it.

Then there were three other women who with great minds and eyes helped with the editing and corrections and spelling. Susan, and (yes, another) Susan and Joan. With out them we really would of lost a lot in the meaning of things.

It would be a true mistake not to mention my three Spirit Guides, Rev. Gladys Custance and Rev. Marion Proctor, along with Brother

Frances, who has been there with much more wisdom than I could ever imagine in the information that is in this book.

Without all this wonderful support, this book would still be on the drafting board just sitting there collecting dust.

Introduction:

(Brother Frances, one of Johns Spirit Guide)

I am glad to be with you this day and send *you* greetings from our world of spirit. We see each of you all the time through all your ups as well as your downs and when you are in need, we make our way to your side and offer support. Many of you experience one of us from the other side at one time or another as you travel on your path of life. If you were to open up your heart to the experience you would know that it was one of us who was there. ***Some of you have doubted the fact that our world does exist and that we are as close to you as the ones that you are friendly with on your side.*** John is a devoted medium and one who truly believes that his work must go on in the right manner and *will* strive to do everything that can be done to carry on the way Mediumship was taught. He is one that is honest in the way it is presented to the public and as accurate as one can receive the message from a Spirit Guide. Not that John is the best in the world, but his belief in the way that words come from a spirit should be presented correctly.

We are very proud to work with him in the creation of this book and in the hope that others will come to an understanding of the work that we do for all of you that reside on the Earth plain. It is true love for you that we come to your world each time. A great deal of the material found in this book comes from us in what you call the spirit world, you will receive not only John's experience of his Mediumship over the years, but ours as well. This work did not come easy to John, like many others, came into this work from different backgrounds and religion influences and through it all some manage to stay with it. There *will* be many things that will be new to you and like many who travel this path of understanding you will either come away accepting what has been told or not, you need to be the judge. However, we ask that you read the text with an open mind and with the hope that your soul will respect the material it contains. We come always in love and *will* walk with you through your journey in life for you never walk alone.

Brother Frances

TABLE OF CONTENTS

MEDIUMSHIP

It is my hope that this book will help you to understand the workings of Mediumship, and that each of you can redevelop the skills that have been dormant for many years, and reopen your communication with your loved ones on the other side. As we redevelop the Mediumistic part of ourselves, our Spirit Guides will be there with us every step of the way, and we should use them whenever we are moved to do so. I always tell my students, if they are asked to serve at churches or other functions, never say no if at all possible. They are advised to call upon their Spirit Guides and go for it! Remember, it is your love for the work and people that you meet, that will allow spirit to help you do the work in a professional manner. If you keep saying no, your guides and helpers will feel that you truly do not want to do the work, and will in time just back away and leave you alone.

The very first thing I want to confess to you is that I came into Mediumship kicking and challenging every word of my teacher and the books I read had to say. I did not want to believe in this, let alone do the work. Coming from a Catholic background it was hard to accept the fact that I or anyone else could communicate with the so-called dead. Several years later I did just that. As a professional I can see the reality of it, and I am glad that I stuck it out, and that my teacher stayed with me in the process of rounding out my knowledge of a new concept.

Let me first say that Mediumship allows more than just a glimpse of the spirit world; it opens the door a lot wider than one thinks. Seeing into this unexplored dimension from which we came allows us to see how the spirit world operates, opening ones eyes to its beauty. As a Medium, you are able to reach out and help so many in need that are still trying to get their lives together. In my twenty or so years as a Medium, I touched so many people who would otherwise still be struggling with the world around them. I give all the credit to my Spirit Guides, one of whom is Gladys. The good work she has done is helping many individuals gain a better understanding of themselves and helping them to find the correct path to travel. My position with the spirit world is one of a receiver relaying its message to the world. Unfortunately, many Mediums take full credit for helping people and neglecting to give crediting to their spirits who guided them. The Spirit Helpers, with their loving devotion and concern, try to make us understand they are here to help us give information from them basic to those on the level at which they live. They are the ones that need more than a "thanks." Again, Mediums are **just** a vehicle acting as a receiving station for spirits to spread their warm influence.

Now that you have a general idea of Mediumship, what is the exact definition of a Medium? Though there are hundreds of definitions that try to explain what does and does not constitute a Medium, there is only one definition that I think has the best grasp of the concept. A Medium is a receiver, it is much like a radio, and you turn to the station that you want. That is what a Medium does - he or she tunes to the right frequency and tunes into his or her Spirit Guide. You have to remember that there are great many spirits out there who want to let you know that they are there. Receiving information from Spirit, the Medium must try to re-transmit it, as that spirit wants it to be told, in a clear and concise manner so the person that the Medium is reading for will understand the message. A reading is made up of conversations between the Medium and the spirit on behalf of the one sitting for the reading. In the past it was called a séance. Like everything else in the world, some Mediums are better than others and the quality of the reading depends upon the ability of the Medium to connect with his or her Spirit Guides and the attitude of the one being read for, along with the Medium's harmony of balance with his or her guides.

There are times, though, fortunately not too many, when a client will come in for a reading with the intent of blocking the reading, and it is the task of the Medium to over-ride that intent and proceed with the reading. So far I have only experienced that twice, and I have had to stop the readings. Similar problems may also come from the other side. One time I recall reading for a lady, and her husband, from the other side, came through in an attempt to take over the reading. Upon stopping the reading I started again and told the Spirit to "back off", which he eventually did. The reading then went smoothly and his wife became a client of mine for a number of years. The job of the Medium is thus not only to give a clear and concise reading, but to maintain control of both the client's intent and that of the spirit that is coming through at the time. Being a receiver is like reading a book on a topic that you choose, but reading it with the thoughts that the Author wanted to relay in each chapter. That is the way the Medium operates on behalf of the spirit that is giving the message. It can be difficult at times to relay the information correctly as it comes through from the other side. It takes a lot of time and training to get yourself to that juncture where the reading **will** be satisfactory to the one for whom you are reading. You maintain a balance between all three: the Spirit Guide, the Medium, and the one being read for.

"HISTORY"

The history of Mediumship reaches all the way back to the time of the bible, and perhaps even predates it. In more recent times, the use of Mediums by prominent people has become much more common, from high-ranking officials in government to professionals at different levels. Even presidents from as early as Lincoln to the ones in such places very recently have utilized Mediums.

Lincoln had a Medium come to the White House on more than one occasion during his presidency.
Nettie Colborne Maynard, the Medium assisting president Lincoln, is fabled to have helped Lincoln win the War Between the States, later writing a book titled "Was Abraham Lincoln a Spiritualist?"

Other notables included Sir Arthur Conan Doyle, the creator of Sherlock Homes and his daughter. Both of whom eventually became Mediums and practiced throughout their lives. According to the "Encyclopedia of Afterlife Beliefs and Phenomena", Conan Doyle was participating in table-turning Séances at the home of the mathematician General Drayson, and became interested in paranormal phenomena, joining the society for psychical research. Doyle embraced the faith of spiritualism after thirty years of study, and started lecturing with his second wife, who also began automatic writing after the loss of her Brother during World War I.

He lectured in northern Europe, South Africa, the United States, and New Zealand and published *"The New Revelations" (191 8)* and *"The Vital Message" (1919).* The Doyles and other forerunners of spiritualism, some entering the ranks with the idea of disproving the reality of Mediumship, themselves became members and true believers of its purpose, allowed Mediumship to grow and flourish into modern times. There are other wonderful people that became famous in their own right, entering the field of Mediumship with the intent of disproving it, but staying for the rest of their lives writing and lecturing, on the subject.

"SENSITIVITY "

Each of us has the ability to sense things or to be in tune with some coming event. A woman that I read for had a dream in which she saw the challenger disaster a few days before it happened. Have you ever picked up the phone to call a friend and have the phone ring? Upon answering, you find it is the person you were about to call. You go shopping, and instead of going to the store that you intended, you go to a different place. There you run into a friend that you have been thinking about over the years as well as recently. You are driving down the street and you go to the right instead of the left in the nick of time to avoid an accident.

My significant other, who is a student in my class, was on her way to a meeting when, in her mind, she saw an ambulance on its way to an accident heading toward, her; then making a right hand turn, going over the median and hitting her car. A second later, this time in reality, she heard an ambulance heading her way and this time she stopped, even though the traffic light was green. The ambulance did make that right turn and headed over the median. There are other similar incidents that people from all walks of life have shared with me over the years. The question that arises is, "are these events coincidences, or are they examples of guidance from our Spirit Guides? These experiences seem to come to us via three different routes. Lets explore these and how a Medium comes in contact with the other side, becoming "in tune" with his or her Spirit Guide. There are many different ways Mediums come in contact with their Spirit Guides. I will go over each of the three ways that were taught to me by my teacher.

There are three main forms or classes:

Clairvoyance
Clair Audience
Clair sentience

Lets first take a look at look at ***Clairvoyance,*** or clear seeing. In this case, a Medium will see a spirit around the individual that he or she is doing the reading for. *It* could be a loved one who has made the transition years ago or even as recently as a year or two ago. *Most* of the time it seems to be a Spirit Guide that came with them before birth, remaining with them until they make their passage back to the spirit world. In Clairvoyance you can also denote special features that will make sense to the one who is being read for. *It* can be some mannerism of the spirit or something unique to the individual so that the one being read for will be able to identify the spirit. Examples of this might include seeing a watch that was special, a ring, or the way the person dressed. Just seeing a spirit is wonderful, and gives you the confidence that they do exist, but a good Medium will also describe the spirit so the person can identify who it is. Relating a name or something special about the spirit, like a reason for passing or other unique information, helps the person listening to the Medium relate to and help identify the entity. This information is what we call spirit verification and it is the job of the Medium to do his or her best in receiving this type of information so that it will validate the reading.

The second type of experience I will discuss is **Clair Audience** or clear hearing. Clair Audience is a situation in which the Medium hears the voice from spirit. That voice will be different than any you ever heard before. These voices can be soft like a whisper, or loud and clear, letting you know that they are there with you - like someone saying, "here I am, just listen to what I am saying to you". Sometimes these voices will occur when you are half asleep, or just before you get up in the morning. Sometimes the spirits speak so quickly and indistinguishably that the Medium must ask them to slow down or pause until the Medium can catch up to what they are saying. A lot of the time, several spirits will attempt to come in all at once. It's like us trying to get in to see some famous star, crowding in to the place where he or she is, and attempting to get a glimpse of the person. This is why the Medium has to take control and ask them to wait, each taking its turn coming in. A good Medium is able to both give a reading and converse with the Spirits at the same time. As you might imagine, this is not easy, and if you are sitting there you may think the Medium has **"lost it".** There is only a handful of Mediums that can do this type of work, and here again, it takes time and training to do it the right way.

The next of these abilities is one that most people have without realizing it. Some people think this is just a little voice in their head, and do not want to realize that it is Mediumship. This is called "***Clair Sentience***" and it means clear sensing. In this situation, there is a presence or something we call a "ghost" that may be sensed around a person or in a house where the ghost will visit from time to time. The Medium is not always able to give specific details about the ghost except that it is in the house, and that in most cases it is not harmful. I have been in places where I have sensed a ghost, and in each of the two instances, I know that there was a ghost present, though some may think it was my own imagination. In one of the places that I was visiting, I was going upstairs when I felt a presence with me. When I reached the landing, I could get the sense of a child coming towards me. Later I found out that the child was a little girl who was killed by a car in the early thirties while crossing the street next to the restaurant to get her father. I had another experience in the case of ghost and spirit communication that was quite interesting to say the least. One night I was at a building by myself and as I was walking through the construction site, I had a feeling that someone was there with me and was not of the physical world. My hair stood on end, and I called my guides to come forth to help, which they did. I must admit that I was a little on edge not knowing what or who was there with me.

"TRANCE MEDIUMSHIP"

One of the forms of Mediumship that is rarely done these days is trance Mediumship. This is a state in which spirit takes over the control of the physical body of the Medium at the time of the reading and **will** speak using the Medium's vocal cords to relay the message. This allows the words of the spirit to come directly from the spirit, and the Medium is not even aware of what is said at the time of the reading. This form of Mediumship is one that is done under controlled conditions and with the aid of an experienced Medium after years of working together. In fact, there are a lot of Mediums that will not take the time to study trance Mediumship (including me) because of the time it takes to learn the skills. There is also a question of whether there is a real need for it today.

I have met several Mediums, who think they can do this without the necessary training that goes with it, and as a result they fool only themselves but not others in the process. There is also a likelihood of the Medium's students and the public getting caught up in it the seeming showmanship, getting the wrong impression of how serious this type of Mediumship truly is. There are Mediums that will not venture into these areas because they know that it takes a great deal of preparation and time in order to do it right. Besides, there may not be much of a need for this type of skill today.

"LIGHT TRANCE MEDIUMSHIP"

Another form of Mediumship, in which the Medium has full control of what is going on and is not under the physical control of the Spirit Guide that is with him or her, is known as "Light Trance". The Medium is just under a slight veil of the spirit influences at this time, and there is no harm to either the Medium or the Spirit. The Medium may have a slight facial change during the reading or other signs of interaction with the Spirit presence. The voice of the Medium may change during the reading, indicating that a spirit presence is there with the Medium.

"RAPID MEDIUMSHIP"

This form of Mediumship is done at a fast rate by Mediums with a great deal of accuracy, as rapidly as their Spirit Guides will allow. Not many Mediums practice this form of Mediumship, either in public or private readings. When this method of presentation is used, it looks as though the Medium is going so fast that he or she cannot catch their breath.

" MEDIUM vs. PSYCHIC "

A student asked me a question the other day, about the difference between a Medium and a Psychic. I looked at him with a look that said, "What is your problem?" I forgot that I had been a professional for a long time, and I guess I just expected him to know that answer. It shows that we as teachers must remember when we ourselves were students sitting in those chairs some time ago, with the picture of puzzlement written on our faces. One question that comes up all the time in different groups where I have lectured is, "What do you do for a living?" When I tell them, in a kidding manner, that I receive messages from dead people it really gets their attention!

Returning to the student's question, there are as many forms and devices of giving readings to others in the mainstream of life today, as there were in the past. These include reading of cards, Crystal Balls and Astrology. Even the different Internet services on your computer have sites dedicated to Astrology, Numerology and other such subjects, which means that you can look up and check your daily forecast or your destiny in an instant. These things are interesting, but for a good and more beneficial reading you should go to someone that is known in the field, whether it is a Psychic or Medium. There are great differences between Mediums and Psychics, but perhaps the greatest difference is the fact that Mediumship involves a direct communication with spirit without the aid of any tools or devices such cards, Crystal Balls, Numerology or the like. This gives Mediumship a uniqueness all its own. Psychics tune into the "vibrations" or other aspects of the persons for whom they are reading, rather than communicating with spirit. As you can see, Mediumship stands alone and belongs in its own category.

With a few Mediums recently coming forward in the media, either reading or lecturing on Spirit communication, and the increasing number of books written on the subject of Mediumship, there is a growing interest within our society. People from all walks of life now become involved in learning more about Mediumship and how it works, as well as acknowledging that perhaps there is something to it after all. I found that a great many people are interested in talking with their loved ones who passed into the other side of life, perhaps asking for forgiveness or seeking some understanding of what the "other" side of life is all about. Another motivator is a desire to somehow relieve the fear of death knowing that we do live on, even if it is in a different place.

Some will come for a reading to find out how their loved ones are doing in their new world and if they linked up with other members of the family that passed. There are some mothers who lost children at birth and because of their loss, held the guilt over the years wondering if they had something to do with the loss. I found that in most cases the mother is not responsible for the loss of the child. The child has the choice to come to the Earth or not. My guides mentioned to me that even at an early age, the soul has the right to make changes just as we do now in our maturity and at out particular stations in life.

"Honesty"

I made a pact with Gladys, my guide, to be honest with my clients, and to give the exact information that comes in from spirit and not to just give the things that will make a person "feel good". Too many Mediums will give a reading that contains only what the person wants to hear, and not the truth. This is not fair to the client or to the guide doing the work. Being accurate in the reading with the client and not allowing the Mediums own information into the reading is important, ensuring the client receives the truth in the way it is given from spirit. Simply seeing a spirit around a person is significant, but one must give the information about that spirit so that the person receiving the reading **will** understand who is there with them. Having humility while doing the reading is also what is expected from the reader. Always give credit to the ones that are doing the work, my spirit guides that are always with me. These are the qualities that I try to maintain with my clients and I will not deviate from them even if the reading is perhaps not what the person wants of experts. Perhaps it is what the person needs at the time. I recall reading for a group of people one night, and it was enjoyable to say the least. One member of the group, a woman, came in with all the expectation of being told that what she was going to do was right and good for her in the long run, and that life would go well for her. Unfortunately, this was not the case. My guide had a different idea, one that the person sitting for the reading would not likely enjoy. I tried to use a little understanding with it however the truth is the truth! After the reading a friend told me that I had been right, and that others had told her that what she wanted to do would not work. It is important to the confirmation of a reading and to know where you stand, even if you did not tell the client what he or she wanted to hear. I don't believe in what I call "flowering" a reading, that is, telling the person that "all is going to go well" in his or her life, if that is not what is going to happen. I know that if I ever did that, my guide, Gladys, would **kick** me all over town!

MY GUIDE, GLADYS

My mother was from Canada, was brought up in a strict catholic family, and had a nephew who became a priest. My mother had to work at an early age, so she secured a job in a candy store on the island on which she lived. One day, one of the inhabitants came in and gave her a reading from cards that he had with him. As a young girl, I am sure that she just "pooh-poohed" it as most young people would have done, but a few years later what was told to her came to pass.

My Mother told me the story, but for a long time I just didn't think much about it or the possibility that this type of thing could really happen. I was young and happy just running a well-established, old family insurance business. Like all businesses, it had its share of problems and challenges, and was having a great deal of frustration just trying to get used to my new role as head of the organization. To add more fuel to the fire I was having problems with the manager that was in the business with me and was having difficulty comprehending the complexity of the things that I had to know. I felt pretty set in life, and was well-established in the way people saw me in the business world. The business itself was doing quite well, and the people in our small town accepted me as a businessman of means, following in the family footsteps. But I was still uncomfortable.

Taking the recommendation of a friend who was interested in Mediumship and the help that it had to offer others and remembering my mother's story. I decided to seek out Rev. Gladys Custance, a well-known and respected Medium in the New England area, who had a small church snuggled in the town of Onset (Cape Cod) Massachusetts. After some hesitation and a lot of skepticism, made an appointment and drove to her home to the Cape. I am known for my punctuality with my clients so naturally arrived at the house with time to spare. Still full of doubts about this "spooky" world of spirits, ghosts and the rest of the things that went along with it, I pulled in to her driveway, and was impressed with the little white house and its charming surroundings. The house had a white picket fence that surrounded the property, and was built in the typical Cape Cod style that was prevalent in the area. I was expecting something quite different, like perhaps a black house with a black cat waiting at the door. With anticipation and apprehension, I knocked on the door, and within a minute, the door was opened by a sweet, pleasant, little elderly lady with an expression of total compassion on her face. I found myself face-to-face with Reverend Gladys Custance; the

Medium who would forever change my path in life.

She invited me inside. Her home was charming, and had a large picture of a man, the "Abbot", who was her guide as I later learned. Once she started the hour-long reading, became amazed by her accuracy. I was intrigued by how someone could know all this information about me, using only a Spirit Guide, who I could neither see nor hear, and without any psychic aids. I thought she might have a spy in my neighborhood, so she could obtain the knowledge of the personal things she spoke to me about. Although the very first reading was a little hard to believe, I returned to Gladys for subsequent readings after some encouragement from my wife. Those readings, in time, made me a true believer of Mediumship and spirit communication. After some time spent in exploring the work, I decided to take the classes that were offered by her and other teachers. They called these classes' "development" classes, which had to do with learning how to tune into your spirit guides.

I didn't want to just jump into Mediumship without searching for what might be a trick hiding in it, so I spent some time trying to disprove this thing called Mediumship. I spent many hours reading books on the topic and seeking answers to my questions that might disprove the concept of Mediumship and its history. At the time, I was still a Catholic, and had a lot of religious philosophy still ingrained in me. In fact, I had so much faith in the Catholic religion that I was, in my early life, interested in perhaps entering the priesthood. My strong religious convictions led me to harbor a lot of skepticism in any other religion or spiritual belief. I never thought that I would make such a drastic change. Upon reflection, I can see what Gladys, as my teacher, was doing in the work and saw the potential in me. There was one thing about Gladys, if she asked you to do something such as going to the podium to do readings (Mediumship), you could only refuse three times. You were never asked again. She knew the potential in her students, and worked with them to bring it out. That is why, in her classes, she worked me as hard as she did during the process of developing the skills of Mediumship. Gladys knew who was ready to do the work, and who needed a little more time. She would do everything she could to develop each student to his or her full potential. She knew when you were dropping from Mediumship into a psychic awareness, and made a point of correcting it right then and there. Let me explain on thing, each step of learning Mediumship is called a *level*. Starting out in Mediumship you work more on a psychic level at first, and in time, move to a level at which the spirits are doing the readings, not you. At first, working on a psychic level is one of the first steps of developing your Mediumship. At this stage you may deviate to the other level very quickly, and it will have an effect on the one doing the reading. For example, one Sunday evening, while serving the church as lecturer and giving messages (giving readings to the people in the congregation), I was about to start reading for the next person, when Gladys, sitting in back of me, said, "that will be the last one." I turned to her and said, I can do another." I proceeded to read and then, without warning, felt completely drained, with not enough energy to finish the reading. Gladys later told me that I had started to work at a psychic level, not as a Medium, and that it had taken the winds out of my sails. I was deflated, but it was a good lesson, and one to remember. Today I keep a close check on my students so they will stay in the appropriate level of the work.

Another one of my teachers was reverend Marion Procter, who also demanded the best of her students. She was both an elementary school teacher and skating instructor in the Boston area. Both Marion and Gladys strived to be the best vehicles for Mediumship, and instilled that drive in their students, bringing out the best in each.

I clearly recall doing readings in class for practice. When I came to Marion in an attempt to give her a reading, she was watching me like a hawk to ensure I would not make any mistakes in my reading. Things were going well until I mentioned that I had a "Mary" with her in spirit. She asked me to identify the Mary that was with her, because there were three Mary's that she knew. I paused for a minute and tried to listen to my guides for the right answer, which I then gave to her and sat down. Her interruption had made me stop, look and listen. As a Medium I do everything I can to encourage my students, and use constructive criticism when necessary (but not to discourage them or them stop doing the work in Mediumship).

My teachers taught that if you were in tune with spirit, you could read for as many people as were in front of you. In the church setting, this was expected - all under the scrutiny of the ministers and members of the church. This process of reading for many persons is not easy, so I do every thing I can to walk the students through the process, helping and encouraging them along the way. Helping them is easy, because I remember sitting there in the class as a new student, trying to fathom all this "new and different stuff", as I would call it.

Gladys taught me many new aspects of Mediumship, and one of her classes dealt specifically with *Phychometry.* This involves holding a tangible object of another person (i.e., keys or a ring) and tuning into the vibrations of the item. Using this method, the reader receives impressions about the person that he or she would not know otherwise. If you think of the process, it's like tuning your television to the station that you want to see, the same things applies to the use of Phychometry. All you are doing is tuning into the individuals channel, or "vibration" and receiving images of things about that person. Before I ever set foot on Gladys' front steps, I had been introduced to the use of Phychometry years ago. At the time, I was just seeking to fill a little time, and to get away from the pressure of my business and the people associated with it, so I took a class on Phychometry and other related new-age concepts. The classes were quite interesting, and I was amazed with what could be seen through the use of Phychometry, and what I myself could see. Perhaps this was one of the reasons I became drawn to Gladys' doorstep that year.

One evening, while attending the class on the uses of Phychometry and developing other skills, we had an exercise in which we paired off with another person and used their rings or other piece of jewelry to give readings to each other. It was at this time that a breakthrough occurred. Both my partner and I were new at this type of reading, but when I took her ring and held it between my fingers I began to see images as though I were watching a miniature television show of her life. The images became so clear that, when I was discussing my images, the woman looked at me and said, "you must know my husband", although I did not know her husband (or even her for that matter). I remember that she called the teacher and asked her if she had said anything to me about her situation. I believe they were having marital problems at the time, and I was tuning into it. The significant fact about the reading was that I was completely accurate. Later, during my growth in Mediumship, I found that Phychometry would be the main focus for helping move a person into the world of Mediumship and that it would have a great effect on their development. Now I use Phychometry in every class from New England to Florida, even teaching it in England. Not only does it work well and help develop the students' abilities more quickly, but it also is an exercise the students enjoy doing.

There are other skills that will help students to develop their Mediumship abilities, and one such skill is meditation. In this approach, you reach a state of consciousness that blocks out the things around you, including your own thinking, and you thus become more in tune with both your inner-self and your Spirit Guides. In this state, you can reach the world of spirit and the loved ones that dwell there, and it is a wonderful experience. There are ways that you can bring yourself to the Meditative state no matter where you are. Another great benefit of meditation comes when you start feeling at peace with yourself and are better able to deal with the hassles of daily life. Meditation takes time to master and the road to mastery can be rough. It is worth learning, if your serious about developing your skills as a Medium.

I continue to have a great deal of respect for Gladys, and the way she was honest in her work with her Spirit Guides and the people for whom she read. She taught that being honest and accurate in your work as a Medium was the only way to go. I endorse this philosophy, and try to maintain that posture in my readings, as well as teaching my own students to do the same. When I reflect on my experiences during my humble beginning as a Medium, I am thankful I had such a wise and compassionate teacher. I remember Gladys conveying to us that we, as Mediums, are only vehicles for the expressions from the spirit side of life, relaying this information back to the one being read for. That is all we are. She cautioned us not to take credit for the messages the spirit was sending, because we were not creating the message - only relaying it.

Another thing I learned was that the best way to give the message is exactly as it comes through from spirit, and not to flower it or make it sound good so that you look like a hero in the process. It is upsetting to me, but there are some Mediums who only give you the good news and leave out the rest of the message that the individual should know, so they can make some corrections in their lives. I don't think they are doing it maliciously, but only want to spare the persons feelings. It is important to convey the full message, because there might be a problem that needs to be addressed in a timely manner, and the person has a right to know. I have read for many people that just want the truth in the reading without giving them just the good news. They feel, as I do, that by distorting the full message you are fooling with their lives. In the readings that I have given, my guides will be direct with the intent of giving people the truth, helping them to see which way they should travel in life. When I myself go for a reading that is exactly what I look for from a Medium - to receive the truth and not just be told that every thing is good and that I should not worry. The correct message can give me the chance to make some needed changes in my life.

One evening, a young couple came in for a reading, the man was quite tall and very strong, and his wife was petite. One of the things they asked was if they could be together for the rest of their lives. My guide came in and said; "no."

then my guide left and I had to explain to them the meaning of the message. Thankfully, the boyfriend, who was larger than I, understood the spirits message and my explanation. Thank heavens! On another day, I received a call from a woman with some major problems and she wanted to come in for a reading. She told me that she had gone to another reader, and the reader told her that she had a curse on her and that she could get rid of it for only ninety-nine dollars. I told her that I felt she did not have a curse on her, but if she wanted the curse removed, I would remove it for a cup of coffee! Unfortunately there are still a few people willing, to take your money in order to rid you of whatever may be weighing on you, and still call the process a professional approach to helping people in need. I know that if I ever attempted to do this, my guide Gladys would give me one swift kick you know where! Many good Mediums out there will "take it on the chin" for the few bad ones like the reader I just mentioned, and this is a shame. Thanks to Gladys and others like her, there has been an educational restructuring, so that students can obtain the best knowledge on subjects that they want and need. Ethics is an important part of the educational process, and thankfully, the practice of making the reading sound wonderful to obtain extra money and to avoid disappointment to the person is becoming a thing of the past. Since the education of

Mediums is an ongoing process and many Mediums continually work on their own ways of developing themselves to be more in tune, this movement is a positive step in the realm of Mediumship.

A good friend of mine is a conscientious and respectable Medium who is well known throughout the world for spreading the word on a professional level. We need more of these Mediums out in the world so people will understand that Mediumship is not a "*gimmick*" but a profession. Over the years, Gladys became my mentor in the work of Mediumship as well as a friend. It was only much later that I realized she pushed me to the limits to help me achieve the highest level of success in my Mediumship and, perhaps, to get me to go out and teach others. In the redevelopment process of Mediumship, (she believe that all of you were born with the ability to be Mediums) the student becomes extremely sensitive, and only a patient teacher understands just how far to push each student, so he or she can attain his or her best, and can truly make a difference.

Yes, Gladys had a gift for that. However, at times, she would push a little too far! Further complicating matters at the time was the fact that I still harbored issues about my previous religion and my upbringing that would create enough inner tension to get some of the hairs on my back to curl. She pushed me further and harder, I had to deal with these issues. When you no longer believe in the way you were brought up, you want change. But you are not quite sure what changes you want to make. You know what you believe and what you don't believe in. Now the challenge is finding the right belief system.

When Gladys eventually made her transition into the world of spirit, I knew we remained connected. One day while taking a walk, I had this flash of Gladys for no apparent reason. Upon returning home, I received a call that she had passed away. The Spiritualist community was shocked, and realized that we not only lost a friend, but a great teacher as well. Now the old-time teaching was gone, but I was hoping that it was not lost forever.

As time had its way, I continued my education in Mediumship, completed the necessary examination and became a certified as a Medium. Eventually, I set up my own classes to instruct others in the work and then, after being ordained as a minister, opened a church near my hometown. I was attempting to follow the path that Gladys would have wanted for me, and to carry on her teaching. I set up my classes the way that I had been taught, and people that came enjoyed it very much. My students, on more than one occasion, told me that they knew that Gladys was a strong presence with me. I would respond by saying, "she is welcome," but I believed that my students were just trying to make me feel good.

It wasn't until Gladys' husband, Kenneth, who is also a Medium and Minister, served my new Church and gave me a reading, that I began to truly believe Gladys was with me. In my reading, he mentioned that she was with me in spirit. He would not deal with Gladys that way unless she was there with me. It was then that I realized that Gladys was truly working with me, and continues to do so to this day. That explains why my readings over the years have been very blunt - that was her style. I used to apologize to people I was reading, for because of the bluntness of the message, but people would chastise me for apologizing, and told me that they wanted and needed to know the truth, no matter how much it might hurt. They would continue by saying that they are sick of other readers telling them every thing is fine in their lives, when they knew there were problems.

Over the years, I have be doing telephone readings, sometimes, at great distances. I have also done radio readings, where the caller calls the radio station and asks for a reading over the air. These, to me, are wonderful opportunities, where more people can gain a clearer an understanding of the work, and learn that there is nothing wrong with Mediumship, as others would have them believe. One of the jobs of the Medium is to help others if they want or need to be helped, giving them the necessary tools to get to where they want to go. This gives me the necessary encouragement to go on with my work in a professional manner. To this day, I know that Gladys continues her work with me, and I hope that she stays with me forever. She and I have a lot to do!

"YOUR LIGHTS ARE ON"

Your lights are on? No, not your car lights or the house lights, but your human " light", your Aura. Your Aura is the light that is on all the time; it is the glow that people see. The Aura is your own personal energy field that encompasses you from head to toe. Auras have been seen and described for centuries in many parts of the world and have been captured in art that adorns the walls of great cathedrals. They may be seen in a wide range of painting, raging from the Christ child to Mary and many other saints. We're not talking about a Phenomenon that just "*popped up*" in recent years, Auras that have been represented in drawings and explained in the writings of ancient civilizations such as Egyptian, Roman, Greek, and Indian cultures.

In the nineteenth century, Dr. Kilmer, an electrotherapist, invented a machine for seeing the Aura around the human body and other objects of interest. Later, Semyon Davikovich Kirlian, a Russian *electrician,* had obtained photographs of the energy field we now call the Aura. He began studying the different patterns that the Aura formed as it emanated from people, plants and animals. Having both studied and taught about the Aura, I realize that the Aura is not a random pattern of Beautifully emanating colors, but that it has its own meaningful spectrum of colors that the human eye can see. Interpreting the Aura in the way spirit directs you is of great value in understanding the person you are reading for, and it never lies, if read properly. There is a great deal of knowledge within the Aura and the shapes and colors that radiate from the person. Like a blueprint of the person, it is all recorded in the auric field.

But I must confess, that for a long time, I could not see the Aura, let alone the colors that encompass it. This was a disappointing reality for an aspiring Medium. It was only after I came to Florida that I was able to denote its full meaning, brilliant colors and the way it was being emitted. It has been exceedingly helpful for me to not only see the Aura, but, thanks to my Spirit Helpers, I am now able to read it. It makes my Mediumship complete.

People of all walks of life can see the Aura around everything like rocks or plants, all the time, without even blinking an eye. I think that it is a great gift. Gladys, my teacher, could see the Aura around people and knew what mood you were in at the time and if you had any problems that were weighing you down. In her classes she taught how to read the Auras. She set up a white sheet and a student sat in front of it so that other students could see that person's Aura a little more clearly without distractions. Then, asked the students to try to see the colors and other distinguishing features present in the subject's Aura and tell her what they saw.

This is a good way for students to tune into the auric field and denote the vastness of the shapes and colors that it has to offer. It also gives the students the chance to expand their abilities. When I was still a student in her class and it came time for me to sit in front of the class, I would make the motion of cranking something up before I sat down in front of the sheet. Gladys would ask what I was doing? I responded, "I am cranking up the Aura. Of course, the class would start laughing and I would get an interesting look from her. She knew I was kidding, but she chastised me anyway.

There are people that say Aura reading is part of being a psychic; however I feel that the spirits give the Medium the information he or she needs, and the patterns, shapes and various colors so that the Medium can decipher the meaning and impart it to the person they are reading for. In this way it becomes a tool for both spirit and the Medium to use for the reading of the person. As for myself, I can see the Aura just enough so that my guides at the time will tell me rather I am right or wrong about that person. Then they will give me the information I need to relate to them. I usually will talk to my guide first before giving the information out. That way I do not come across wrong to the person I am reading for.

Some Medium's, like myself, will only give the basic colors of the Aura while other Medium's are able to give the full spectrum of the colors. There are three ways to detect the Aura. I will review each one so you will understand some of the ways a Medium tune's into the person's Aura.

First, let's begin with the Medium actually seeing the Aura, with its dazzling variety of colors, shapes and sizes, that is very much part of us. These colors and shapes will, if read properly, tell a great deal about the person and what is happening in his or her life at the time. There are a few Mediums I know that can actually see the Aura and its array of colors, and be able to interpret what they see. As I previously mentioned, my teacher, Gladys, could see the Aura with great clarity and most people could not fool her even if they wanted to. There are times that a student would go to her class and would appear to be quite happy and Gladys would make the comment that the student was not "up to par", and that there was something weighing on his or her mind.

One of my other teachers that I had great respect for was Reverend Marion Procter, a tough lady to get to know, but another one of the teachers that expected a lot from her students. She could not only see the Aura, but also draw it in charcoal, using paper in your choice of color, showing the Aura as it appeared to her while you were sitting in front of her. The thing that was particularly interesting about this is that the color paper you chose would reflect your spiritual path in life at that time. Marion did an Aura drawing for me on a blue background with beautiful detail of the different shapes and colors she saw in my Aura. I still have it hanging on the wall of my home to enjoy and show people who are interested in the Aura.

I have to say, she did a great job with my Aura, showing all the colors - from whites to greens - that were illuminating from me at the time. The colors in her depiction seem to flow out from my body and up rather high, turning in different directions forming a pattern as unique as my fingerprint. When I asked her what the colors meant, she told me that I would understand in time, and as time went on, I did understand a great deal about myself through the Aura. The ability to see Auras varies from person to person. I have come along way in my understanding and sensing of the Aura as I work in my Mediumship.

While there are some that see the Aura all the time and can not shut it off because it comes naturally to them, there are others for whom it takes a lot of patience and practice to even start seeing the Aura, let alone the colors. While I was teaching a class on the Aura one day, one of my students could see the Aura in great detail around people all the time, and had a hard time shutting it down so that she could have a normal life. I also had a student that had a very difficult time seeing anything that remotely resembled an Aura around anything, let alone a person. I could tell that she was getting a little frustrated and almost ready to give up. I worked with her in the class by asking her what she was seeing at the time and finally she was able to see a little of the colors and shapes of the Aura. Some time later she mentioned that she could see the Aura a lot better then she did in the class, and that she is still working with it. It takes time to develop your skills for reading the Aura as it does for every thing that you want to accomplish.

The second way to detect the presence of the Aura is sensing the Aura around a person. I believe that this is the manner in which most Mediums tune into the Aura then depending upon what their spirit helper says about the Aura, they will relate it to the person getting the reading. The way it was explained to me, the Medium receives an impression of the Aura in his or her mind and then relays the message back to the other person. This impression includes the colors and other important information about the person seen in the Aura. It sounds a little complex, but it gets easier, depending on how long you and your Spirit Guide have been working together and your receptiveness to your Spirit Guide at the time. One of the problems with sensing the Aura rather than seeing it, is that you may think that your imagination is at work, and not that you are actually being directed by spirit. Be careful to learn the difference, but be confident that you will learn to sense both the Aura and your Spirit Guide at work.

When I read Auras, I always mention to my clients that what I tell them about their Aura is my Spirit Guide's interpretation of the colors. To explain, if I see the color purple around a person, my interpretation would be that healing was associated with this person. Depending upon the direction in which the energy is flowing, either the person can heal others or they are receiving healing. If the color is flowing out of the person, he or she is healing someone else. Also the depth of the color will indicate whether the person is a strong healer or not. By the way, the more that one uses the energy, the stronger it becomes. That also applies in Mediumship.

The third and final way to detect the Aura is "feeling" the Aura itself. Feeling an Aura without visually registering it happens more often that you think. Have you ever walked into a room full of people and felt that you wanted to stay away from someone, or even a few people in particular? Or, have you walked into the same situation and had a good feeling about the group without knowing why? You are in contact with the collective Aura of the group, or group Aura. As you have the opportunity to meet the people individually, you will also tune in to their Auras and will feel or sense of something about that person. When you stop and think about it; that's neat! But don't forget that both of you are coming in contact with each other's Auras. Both of you will gain impressions of many things from the energy field, the Aura, that encases the person you are with. So, the next time you attend a group of some kind, stay in tune with your Aura and let it guide you. See what you pick up. How do you react to a person and how that person reacts to you? You will be surprised with the information revealed to you. Once you understand the working of the Aura, it will never let you down.

Now that I have explained how people sense the Aura, I would like to discuss what they are seeing, or sensing, and the meaning and interpretations that go along with it. The shape and size of the Aura is important, as there are many different configurations. Most Auras extend, or radiate, between two and three feet from the human body and have an egg-shaped appearance. If a person is extremely energetic and constantly active in his or her daily life, the Aura will be extended way out from the body. Conversely, the Auras of people who are very unsure of them self are thin and tightly wrapped around their bodies. Instead of shining from the person, the Aura looks more like light is enveloping the body of the person in a very close compact manner.

While visiting us in Florida, my daughter, Ann, and a college friend were asked to participate in one of my classes on seeing and interpreting the Aura. They came with me to one of the places I was doing readings. After the readings, one of the owners of the place came over to chat with us. After he left, my daughter commented that she could see the color black around him and felt that he was a person to stay away from. I had the same feelings about him. Interestingly enough, this was the first time that my daughter did any work with Auras, and we were in compliance with one another. She could see a great deal of the Aura around a person; better than I did on my first day of those years in training.

The shape of an Aura can also reveal a lot once you become used to the shapes and textures of the Aura. If it is smooth, it means that the person is relatively healthy and that all is going well in his or her life. As long as the Aura is maintained in that way, the person will remain in that good condition. When I see jaggedness or roughness in the Aura, it means that there is some problem in the person's life. The problem can be depression, health issues, family problem or an array of other situations that need to be addressed so that the person can go on with the correct path in life. There are Auras that have what look like tears in the surface of the Aura. These tears have some significance and must be taken into account when reading the Aura. The tears mean that there is healing to be done with the person, and that these health problems need to be addressed. It is up to the Medium, with the Spirit Guide, to make the interpretation of what is seen, and to assist the person that they are reading for.

I saved this for last because it is very important and warrants a little more time so that you can get more understanding. There have been so many books written on the colors of the Aura, that there is no reason why a person cannot gain in-depth knowledge of the subject from one source or another. There are many that will disagree with what I am about to share with you, and that is okay, for the idea is to look at other opinions that are available. I admit that the longer I have been doing this work, the more convinced I am that each Medium has his or her own interpretations of the colors in the Aura based on what their guides tell them.

What I was taught, and what my Spirit Guides relate to me, is a little different from the way other Mediums learned to interpret the Aura. That is fine, as long as the help is right for the person that they are reading for. I am one that only sees the basic colors in the Aura and that is fine, for my Spirit Guide gives me the needed impressions. I know my guides will help me to interpret the colors to help my client receive the necessary information. I am sharing with you my interpretations of what my spirit guides convey to me about the colors of the Aura and their meanings for each individual. The colors seen in an Aura also contain clues to the person it surrounds like a fingerprint of that person. For example, there are a few people that have black and gray hued colors in their Aura that definitely denotes a deep, hidden unhappiness in themselves. These colors notify the Medium that the person probably feels down and needs the help of a healer to lift them back up. People with bright colors are more vibrant and happy with themselves and their lives, which is where we all need to be.

The basic colors of the Aura that I will discuss are:

- Red
- Yellow
- Orange
- Green
- Blue
- Pink
- Purple
- White

The first of the colors Red: represents energy of the people, either in the way that they act or think. These people are going on a fast pace in their lives. These people have a hard time keeping in a relaxed mode and find it hard to sleep at night. If the color red is entering them from spirit, then they need more energy entering their lives, and if it is coming from spirit they should be moving right along.

The color Yellow denotes joy. The individuals are in a good state of being and feel comfortable about their progress in life. The color Yellow, as you might expect, is hard to see around people today, and that is a shame, because we should feel good about ourselves more often than not.

The color Orange: represents wisdom. The color orange is something most people, myself included, wish they had more of in life. Persons with this color in their Auras have the potential to be very successful in whatever they do. They should, however, remember that most of this wisdom and insight comes from spirit and not from what they have learned through the years in class. Again, if the color orange is exiting the person, it means he or she is passing this needed wisdom to others through teaching or writing - things that are of great interest to the general public if you go to the local book store you will see books on a spiritual nature written by people that are in the process of expanding their minds and exploring new approaches to what the universe is all about. Interestingly enough, some of the great literary authors had orange in their Auras. Maybe they tapped into their Spiritual wisdom to create their masterpieces.

People usually associate the color Green with money or security. To me, when seen in an Aura, it represents security in the form of finances or in themselves as a person.

The color Blue signifies the spiritual essence of a person, not always the religious path, but more the true "self" of their spiritual nature. A person with this color has a spiritual quality about them, and you will most likely sense it when he or she enters the room. Most people with blue in their Auras either know they are especially spiritual, or subconsciously deal with themselves on a spiritual level, not realizing the potential they have. The people I have read for over the years have enough blue around them so that my guides relate to them that they should start developing their gift or perhaps turn to the spirit side of life. Both my guide and I sincerely hope that they will.

The next color is one that at times amuses me when I see it. This primarily happens when a man comes in for a reading and I see a lot of this color in his Aura, even though he thinks he is too tough for it, of course I am talking about the color Pink. This wonderful color reveals the true sensitivity of the people. To me, pink represents love and affection, and the meaning varies with the intensity of the color seen in the Aura. Many people with pink in their Aura want to release it and snare it with others. Some have more difficulty with this than others. Along the same lines, I think readings for men are fun in that they often want to cover up their true feelings. A lot of that no doubt has to do with the way the person was brought up. Most men will come for a reading under the pretense that a wife or significant other "asked them to do it". You might call it a protest, big time! I was in the same boat before I became actively involved and understood what other men go through. Even I had to deal with it. But that does not change the realization that when they are there before you with a look of "watch out - I don't believe in this stuff", both you and your guard must be on guide and ready for any thing that the person might say.

One evening I read for this tall young man who wanted to check me out before sending his fiancée up for a reading. That's okay, because it is good to be curious. This kid had to be at least six feet tall and appeared capable of handling himself in any situation without any problems at all, including whatever I might say. He had a lot of hidden pink around him and had a difficult time trying to release it in his new relationship. Later, he told me he was a New Jersey state police officer. As in this instance, I have read for many men who came to me with all the resentments they could muster and a nudge from their respective spouses. During the course of the readings, good old emotions kick in, and their true colors come bursting through their Auras. When the color pink is one of the main colors, it becomes very expansive. I tell them they are holding too much in and are ready to explode with emotions; like keeping your finger over the mouth of a soda bottle and shaking it up. The same applies with each person emotional level-we must express our emotions, or we will feel the negative effects of not doing so. You can see the emotions, in the form of tears, starting to roll down the cheeks of the biggest of men. Pink is a wonderful color, and most of the people that I have read for over the years have turned out to be a bundle of love, including myself and the other men of the world.

If pink denotes sensitivity, then the next color, Purple implies healing. Many people have purple in their Auras without knowing it or the potential they have in doing healing. As I sit here writing this book, I recall that one of my favorite colors as a child was purple, and now I know why. This color denotes the healing potential of the person and this rich color is prevalent around them quite deeply at times. Again, the ability depends on the direction the color is going when you observe it around a person, if purple is coming to the person then that person is in need of healing. Conversely, when purple is emanating from the person then the person can heal others even though they may not know it. There are times that the person I am reading for will have purple surrounding their arms, at times very bright, and their hands will be quite hot. This is an indication that healing energy is flowing out from the person. The color purple, especially in the Aura, means something very special in the life of the person, which it encompasses.

The final color I will discuss is White. White in the Aura denotes God's consciousness, and it is a superb color to have around you at all times as you travel through life with its rough roads and pitfalls. There are many people that have this color emanating from them throughout their lives, and who use their efforts to help others along the way. The neatest thing about the color is that you can ask for the white light to flow around you and better still, send it to others who are in need (that is just about everyone that you may know). I ask for the white light of protection from God every chance I get, with the sincere hope that God **will** hear me, and I think everyone could benefit from doing this.

I find it interesting that I don't always see the color white swirling around people when I read for them. It doesn't mean that the person lacks the white light; it just means that I cannot detect it around them at the time of the reading. In your personal time of silence, I encourage you to ask God for this white light to enfold you and stay with you forever. White light can help you with understanding the Aura and relying on your Spirit Guide for the help you need in interpreting its shapes, colors and "swishing" effect. This in turn, will help you to better understand the makeup of other people.

So, remember at all times
"That your light is on"!

"SPIRIT, OH SPIRIT, WHERE ARE YOU?"

In my twenty or so years as a Medium, I have had many different questions asked of me on Mediumship, ranging from: "can you contact my father from the spirit side?" To, "how do you do that?" I have found some of these questions very interesting and at times provocative, prompting me to reach way back in my mind for the answers. For others, I have had to ask my guide for help. One of the questions that always come up is, "how do I contact my guide". When I explain how easy it is to contact their Spirit Guides and helpers, they just look at me with a "you've got to be kidding", attitude.

Before I go into the "how", I would like to explore some of the differences between a spirit guide and a spirit helper. We talk or read so much about this subject in the many books that are on the shelves of the many bookstores. First, a Spirit Guide is a spirit entity that has been assigned to you before birth, making the trip with you to the Earth plane and remaining with you until you go back home to the spirit side of life. Over the many years that I've been doing this work, I have learned that a spirit can be assigned to you even if it is not your assigned guide.

This is of great interest to me, for I experienced this with one of my helpers that became assigned to me as a guide later in my life. This helper was one of my teachers who helped me become a Medium, and has been following me ever since. Her name is Gladys. I am sure that she is helping me write this book to help others who might be in the same searching place that I was in years ago.

Next, let us look at Spirit Helpers. Who are they and what is their purpose? For one thing, we have many around us all the time. We might call them our guiding angels without wings. Like the Spirit Guides that each of us have, the helpers are there to assist us as we travel through the Earth side. One of their missions is to help us to learn and grow in our understanding of the Earth and ourselves as its new inhabitants. Now it is true that we have been here before, some of us many times. Upon arrival, however, we forget our experiences of the past. Our helpers will support us in some of things that we need to know about this world as we fulfill our mission here.

Their help may come to us as flashbacks, or what we "call impressions out of the blue" helping us to make those needed decisions about problems that have plagued us. For example, you might be working on some situation, having a hard time finding the solution. One day you come up with the answer - it just pops into your head, and you say, "Where did that come from?" Your spirit helpers are at work, gently giving you the answer that you seek. As your understanding of them and the help that they give you grows, you move to a different and new level of vibrations. As that happens, you will become more aware of your helpers, and will learn to depend on them. These Spirit Helpers will come and go depending on your needs at the time. As things change in your life, so will your helpers. They will arrive, staying with you until the issue is resolved, and then move back until you call upon them again. As you learn to depend on them and other things arise in your life a new helper will come in to assist you. One of the comforting things to remember is that you are never alone. Your helpers are always there for you.

Now that we know that our guides and helpers are with us, how do we call upon them for help?

To the surprise of many, it is not that difficult to contact them or your loved ones. In fact, it is easier than you think. Sometimes it appears too easy, and after you read the explanation you will say, "why didn't I think of that"? Years ago I asked my teacher this same question, only I said, "do you pick up the phone and dial 1 -800-spirit?" Of course, she just laughed at that comment and gave me a strange look, as if to say, "What am I going to do with you?" She mentioned that the way to contact spirit is to simply ask, by mouthing these words three times: **"SPIRIT, SPIRIT, SPIRIT",** to yourself or if you wish, aloud. If a Medium gave you your spirit's name, say the name three times.

Okay, that's not too difficult, is it? Many people will make it seem that reaching your Spirit Guide is extremely difficult, but clearly that is not true. Why would it be, if guides are here to help us, not hide from us somewhere in the corner of the universe. The only difficult part is for us to keep quiet and listen to what our guides are telling us, not letting our own minds get in the way as often happens.

The impressions forming in your subconscious mind are those of the guides coming to help you. In time you will be able to distinguish the differences between your own thoughts and theirs. It will not be as though someone is speaking all kinds of words into your ears, or a loud voice is waking you up at night saying, "Hi, I'm here, wake up and listen to me now or I will go else where with my story of goodness." Rather, the message will be one of gentleness, uplifting support and a great deal of love. Spirit will not tell you what to do, only suggest the way you might look at things before making a move. As you travel through life, you want not to be pulled into things, but to be guided with understanding.

One of the hardest things for most of us to understand is that the guides are really here for us all the time, every day of the week. Most of us have the misconception that our Spirit Guides are out of reach, but in fact they are a lot closer to you than you may think. Their world parallels ours, and at times the two are quite close. What separate us from their world are the rate of vibration and our lack of understanding of them and the world in which they live. In order to understand the world of spirits, we first have to try to peer into its veil that becomes a barrier.

It is like attempting to understand customs of another country, and its people without either going there or reading about it. We tend to form our own ideas without first exploring facts and gaining knowledge about that country, which indeed might cause us to form different opinions.

This same theory applies to the understanding of the world of spirit. In an attempt to get a view of their world, we first have to realize that we are looking into another world very much like our own, except that it is a world of complete harmony, where things are much brighter and more beautiful than in the world in which we live. This is not an easy place to see from our vantage point, and with our human eyes, its like looking into the ocean trying to see the bottom that is several miles down beneath our boat. In the murky water, we know that the sea has all types of dwellers, but we don't know what type of inhabitants are there because all we can see is shadows and movement – not true pictures. It's only when the inhabitants come up to the surface that we see the true form and denote what is there.

The same thing applies to the world of spirit. We cannot fully see with our naked eyes, but with the help of Mediums, the world of spirit will be revealed to us. This world has been revealed to us through Mediumship many times, and has revealed some of its wonders. With the current investigation of NDE (Near Death Experiences), we are getting yet another look into this world, and the reports verify what Mediums have been saying for years through readings and study on this fascinating subject. Over the past few years, people who were clinically dead and then revived, have reported traveling to the other side. They have returned with information about seeing their loved ones, and given us glimpses of the other side. This has been a big help to our understanding of the Spirit world. Both NDE's and Mediumship have increased our awareness of the world of spirit and the peace to which we will someday return.

The more you do Mediumship, the more your guides and helpers will work with you, and in time the in tune you will become. I always do readings when asked to so, and it gives me time to be with my guide. We both learn from the experience, and I always need the practice. This is also true in healing - the more times you work with healing in conjunction with your helpers the more refined you become. A spirit helper will elect to stay with you for many years while you are learning the work in your Mediumship or healing capacities, until it is time for you to go to a new level, at which time a new helper will take over. Your spirit helper knows when you are ready to go to the next level, so never fear that you are not as far along as you think you should be. You will progress at the rate you are supposed to.

Another question that is frequently asked of me is, "can you give me the name of my Spirit Guide?" I tell them that there are times that spirit will not give me the names of the entities that are around, and for all intent and purposes, they are not needed. To know the name of the guide is wonderful if it is given, but knowing that one or more is there with you is what really counts. There are other times when the Medium will get the name of the spirit around a person, perhaps a loved one that passed to the other side years ago. One of the things that is interesting is the fact that when persons pass into the world of spirit, they take their personalities with them. So unless you make some changes now, you will be carrying whatever you are with you when you arrive over there. If people are strong willed here, they will be the same over there, but like here; you can make changes if you want to.

If you are told that you have a master force as your Spirit Guide, you need to ask questions about that guide in order to truly determine just how masterful that guide really is. I don't want you to think that you are not capable of having a high force with you; what I am saying is, there are people that will tell you only things that you want to hear, not what is always true. The really important thing is that your guide is a respectful and honest entity, who will guide you correctly in your life and work with you to accomplish your mission. A woman came to me and told me that she was very lucky to have an archangel with her at all times in her life. She mentioned that no matter how great a problem she had, she could call upon her archangel for help. I knew this woman and what her work was like. If she had an archangel, it wasn't there that day!

Most of us will have great Spirit Guides. They may not be "master forces", but they will be honest and loyal, and will always be with us in time of need. Try not to get hung up in finding out the names of your guides. Just trust in them and believe in them, and know that you have the guide that you need at this time in your life. That is the most important thing you can ever do.

What I hope to teach people, is that when your Spirit Guide speaks to you, please just listen. That also is very hard to do, but very important for a Medium. As I have mentioned before, the impressions that you feel will be from your Spirit Guide and not your own imagination. Your job is to listen, and then use the information so you can travel the rest of your life on a better and more positive road. As you can see, it is not important to know who your guides are - just that they are there, and that you receive the information correctly so you can in turn give the information correctly. My own spirit helper is not a master force, but a very stubborn woman who cares about what I am doing. She assists me in the work, at times quite forcefully, but it helps me get the message across to the person that I am reading for, and she does the same regarding my own personal life. I would rather have someone who gives the best support and most accurate information that the client needs to know, along with the best advice on how to live a better life.

"PROTECTION"

I would like to take a few minutes to discuss what we must do before we start into the work as a Medium, or if you just wanted to contact spirit for help to get you through the day.

It's a process that I do twice a day, and its called "PROTECTION", and it is something, that all Mediums must do in order to do the work. In fact, it's a must for me to do in the morning, after making the coffee, and also do at night, and I try to also do it in the course of the day. I find my quiet spot in the house where there is no noise or commotion of any kind, and start the protection process. In this all-important process, you start by taking a nice deep breath and then just ask for your Spirit Guide or helpers for their help. Do it with a positive tone, as if they were sitting with you in your room (in fact they are). We spend a great deal of time in our prayers asking for help in a solemn manner, when we need to become more positive in our request.

It is fine to go to the top and ask God for protection by saying three times:

"GOD, GOD, GOD, I NEED YOUR PROTECTION AND YOUR WHITE LIGHT TO BE SURROUNDING ME AND ALL OF MY LOVED ONES, ATTRACTING ONLY THE BEST IN OUR LIVES ALL THE TIME, UNDER THE RIGHT CONDITIONS".

As you are saying this, you can picture the white light flowing, around you and all your loved ones, or you can picture a paint can full of white paint pouring all over you and your loved ones. The "white paint" is God's white light of protection. In a short time you will not only feel the peace, but will have the sense of divine protection flooding your consciousness. You can request your Spirit Guide or helpers in the same manner saying:

"SPIRIT, SPIRIT, SPIRIT, I NEED YOUR
HELP THIS DAY TO BE MORE
POSITIVE AND TO HAVE ONLY THE BEST
ENTER INTO MY LIFE, AND TO
HAVE THIS PROTECTION FOR ALL THAT I MEET
THIS DAY".

An interesting point about your Spirit Guides is that they will never leave you, even when you are down in the dumps or as you travel through the tosses and turns life offers you. You are never alone as you walk the winding pathway of your adventure, no matter now difficult it may seem at times. There have been times that even I have doubted my Spirit Guide-its just something we all go through. But you will get the feeling, of the presence of your guide right beside you, with an encouraging message to stay on the path, that all will be well.

There are times that entities will appear without you thinking about it, stopping in to let you know that you are not alone. This happened to me one day while I was preparing for a wedding I had to do in Orlando, Florida. It was a good-sized wedding, and I usually go over the service the day before the wedding, making sure that it runs as smoothly as possible (to avoid Murphy's law). I started to go over the text for the service, when I received a glimpse of a woman from spirit standing right next to me with a warm and caring smile that extended from ear to ear. I knew who it was, turned to her and said, "hi Carol" I turned back to what I was doing and she disappeared. I'm not sure why she was there, perhaps only to let me know everything is going to be okay.

Carol, her husband Peter and I were in the same church in Massachusetts. We became good friends throughout the years of our redevelopment classes and church functions. In our classes we had a good time making the best of things, as we learned to become Mediums. In time, even our teacher Gladys would let her hair down. She explained that even spirit likes to have some fun. After class and a group of us would be invited to join the Gladys's at their home for lunch. She didn't invite everyone, so it was a privilege for those of us who went. Carol and I would sometimes get the job of washing the dishes, and of course I would start teasing her with the encouragement of her husband. Before I knew it, there would be more soap on the both of us than anywhere else. A few years later, Carol made her transition into the world of spirit. We were not only shocked, but all of us who knew her suffered a great loss of a wonderful soul. There are many times when a spirit will visit us, offering help when we are just on the verge of giving up, or when we don't understand which direction to travel. Our Spirit Helpers will come to us because of our auras, like beacons emitting flashes of light that spirit will understand. One day, while outside thinking about a question that was asked by one of my students, my guide came to me and proceeded to give me a gentle nudge about the question and a strong impression about the answer (in other words, "here it is!"). It made perfect sense to me, and now I can tell people who will ask me the same question, an answer that makes sense. This was a great test for me in both the fact that spirit will give me the help I need, and that spirit will be there for me all the time.

There are times when spirits will appear to you without asking for them, as if to say, "I am still with you". Their intent is to let you know that all you have to do is ask, and they will be with you. Several years ago my wife and our two children were living in my grandparents' home that was left to me upon the passing of my grandmother in the late seventies. One morning my oldest boy, nine years of age, came running up the stairs to our bedroom, waking us up out of a deep sleep and telling us of seeing this very tall man downstairs walking through the hall, then walking through the pantry door at the rear of the kitchen. I was not shocked by his report. I had just started my journey into uncharted waters of unexplained happenings in life. Today, I understand that it was my grandfather my son had seen, who dearly loved the old home that he had owned for many years. I had great respect and love for my grandfather and his home. The spirit essence that my son saw that day and described with great accuracy, was a very welcome guest.

There are so many wonderful stories that people told me throughout the years of similar happenings involving spirit entities coming close to them. Letting them know that love has no boundaries and they will be with them as long as they are wanted. As a Medium, I know that for a spirit to come back to the material plane is difficult at best. Those who do, come with love for each of us. The denseness of our world makes the journey a tough trip. They make the sacrifice with devotion to their loved ones they had left behind, and do so with the intent of encouraging us and making our lives a lot better. From what we as Mediums have been told, the other side of existence is a very bright and beautiful one, free of all pressures. Spirits have a total commitment to each other. If we can learn this type of commitment from them, they keep coming back time and time again to help us anyway they can. We should be more than grateful that they do come back to help us when we are in need, bringing with them great joy and happiness. By the spirits making such a trip, they reinforce our belief in the concept of the continuity of life after the change call death, and that they travel on in an other dimension of time and space, in a world much like our own.

"WOW IT WORKS!"

What is very interesting about Mediumship is the fact that working with the spirit world helps me to better understand the workings of those who truly care. It also gives me confidence, in that I am helping others to find their way in life. There is also a great deal of joy in knowing that we as Mediums can help people feel happy about themselves. Each time I am asked to read for a group or an individual, I still am amazed at the results that the messages from spirit can bring about in my clients at the time. Some messages are so accurate that I just sit back in wonderment realizing that whatever my guide gives me I must tell my client whether they may like it or not. I think that people want the truth and not just whatever will make them feel good for a short time. There is no question that working with my guide as a Medium takes a great deal of faith and trust in God, who has put it all together. There are times my guides have a sense of humor, and other times when they are quite stern and very direct about the messages to my client. As I have said before, my guide is a very feisty entity who does not believe in pulling any punches with clients, just giving them the truth. The people that I have worked with enjoy that approach, rather than being led down the wrong path. Before any readings, I ask my Spirit Guide to allow me to be an open and clear vehicle for the work. For myself, I ask to be accurate, honest and humble in my effort to give the client the best reading possible. I always give thanks to my Spirit Guide after the reading.

In the past twenty or so years that I have been a Medium, I have read for many people, from all walks of life from famous to ordinary, and at times it has been challenging to say the least and yet very rewarding. In all these years of doing readings, my Spirit Guide has never let me down-even with the skeptics that come for a reading just to attempt to disprove it (sounds like me when I first started). There are a few clients who will try to block the reading, intending to prove (to themselves) that this reading was inaccurate. In some way this seems to give them more ammunition to say, "I told you so". Many have come in for a reading with that attitude and left with the knowledge that it does work; and that there is something to Mediumship after all. Its even more interesting that they will not only believe, but many will come back at a later date. Some even join my classes at the church. One never knows where or how the interest develops and grows. I was invited one day to speak on the air at a local radio station. It was in the Boston area and it was a lot of fun. I had the chance to read for a lot of people that day over the air. People enjoyed it and the phone lines were all lit at the station. What a wonderful way to reach people.

I have reached out to many people and made a lot of friendships that have lasted over the years. People now call for private readings, phone readings and group readings along with house parties (going to a persons home and doing readings for guests that the owner has invited). One of these house parties lasted for around nine hours and at the end of the evening I was ready to go dancing, except for the fact that I can't dance. My helper Patricia, who was doing the bookings, was ready to go home. That is how spirit works. If you are doing the work from spirit and not from your ego, you are on a high and are receiving a great deal of energy from them. This was not always true when I first entered the field of Mediumship. It took a long time to be able to trust my guides to take over, and for me to just keep my mind out of their way. This is something that takes time to learn, since our minds tend to always get in the way. Most of us just like to rationalize everything. We attempt to place things in a small box and then examine it for flaws.

We were taught this at a very early age, but in Mediumship you cannot think about what you are going to say. There is no script to read. You just give out whatever comes from spirit. That is the true sign of a Medium. As my teacher stated, "when you are ready to study music, you learn to read the notes and the scales. In Mediumship you are taught not even to think...

Just to allow spirit to take over in order to do the work, giving the information the way spirit just gave it to you." Again my teacher was right. We tend to forget what we are supposed to do.

I have passed this information along in my classes, and have seen a great improvement as the students start their redevelopment work in Mediumship. I'm not sure I explained why we use the term redevelopment verses development. We (Spiritualists) believe that you come to the earth with the ability to do Mediumship and it is drowned out of you as you grow. We now feel the term redevelopment is more in tune with reality. To say that this is easy would be just as if I were trying to convince you that I have the Brooklyn Bridge for sale. You know better! You have to stand aside and allow your Spirit Guide to do the talking - not you! I remember one of my readings that taught me this great lesson. I was just a student in Onset, Massachusetts, when I was asked to serve the church on a Sunday evening. It was an honor for me, because you had to be asked by your teacher before you were allowed to do the work from the church podium. In Mediumship demonstration (giving messages) to the members of the congregation, a Medium or student gives each member a message from spirit and also a spirit that they could be related to you, like a father or someone that was close to them. I took my place at the podium and started to do the readings with all the feelings of nervousness that goes along with doing this for the first time. I believe I left my fingerprints embedded in the podium that evening. My teachers always believed that if you are working from spirit you can read for all the people in the congregation, so that meant that if there were fifty people attending, you were expected to go to all fifty and give them a message that was significant.

I started, and all went well until I came to a couple of ladies sitting on the left-hand side of the church under the open windows. I started reading for one of the women when I heard the word from my Spirit Guide telling me that she was going to have a child. I mentioned that to one of the women who spirit pointed out, but both were shaking their heads in a negative way. My heart sank with sheer disappointment, but Spirit was very insistent on the subject to a point that I felt I must stay with it, so I did. The more I relayed the messages from spirit the more both women were shaking their heads and as I recalled they were getting a little irritated with me, but Spirit has a way of sticking to the matter at hand so I repeated it once more and ended with "perhaps you should get a second opinion."

After the service, the woman I had just read for went storming out of the church and her friend came over to me and said: "John, I realize that this is your first time doing public readings my friend was told that she cannot have children." I told her that I was sorry, but my spirit was very insistent on the fact that she is with child. After she left, I went home with the idea of quitting Mediumship and not going to the church. The experience had been that devastating to me. About three weeks had gone by, and I decided to go to one of the evening services at the church, see what was happening, and listen to the lecture. After the service I went up to the guest lecturers to congratulate them on their work for the evening, when a lady came over to me and said, " John, do you remember the reading you gave three weeks ago to a friend of mine? You told her that she was going to have a child!" I mentioned that it was quite an evening! She said, "you'll never guess what happened - she went to another doctor and as you stated, she is pregnant." To tell you the truth, I was a little shocked myself, but happy that spirit was right and that I stayed with the reading the way it came from my Spirit Guide. I was also happy that the woman would have the child that both she and her husband wanted over the years. I looked at her and said, "I didn't do it." We both laughed and she went on her way.

I was extremely impressed with the turn of events, and it gave me the faith and confidence to continue on with the work and never doubted my guides again. Through the years I never questioned my Spirit Helpers and always relied on them for support, both for me personally and in the work as a Medium. Most of the readings have been quite different and interesting, involving subjects such as contacting a loved one that has been in spirit to "What type of work should I do?" People are still interested in reaching their angels and Spirit Guides and will ask me to give them their names and to tell them if these helpers will assist them in their quests in life? I think it is amazing that people are still interested in the search for what some will call the unknown, though to many it is not unknown at all.

I did a reading for a person who wanted to talk to his grandmother who passed some years ago, and he was taken back when I told him that his grandmother was not there for this session. Perhaps she did not want to talk to him at this time. He looked at me as if to say, "you are nuts, that's my grandmother." I explained to him that just as here in the material world, spirits have jobs to do and other people to visit. There was a reason for the grandmother not to be present that day.

She could have been visiting with other relatives or friends on the Earth side that needed her assistance or she just might be somewhere in another level doing other things. Some of the spirits are helping new arrivals that have made their transition into a different vibration of the world of spirit. These new arrivals will have to adapt to their new home and to a new way of life in the spirit world, like if we were to go to another country to stay.

The idea that his grandmother would be at the reading is not always realized. This does not mean that the one you expect to be there does not love you, or just doesn't care. That is not true. Our Spirit Guides and loved ones still love us, and will be with us as much as they can, helping us as we make the transition to the other side when it is our time to go there. It is not uncommon for a loved one to come in towards the end of a reading and say " don't worry I am still with you even if I am late." In one of the readings that I did, the person wanted to reach her mother who passed some years ago and hoped to resolve some issues with the mother. Her mother was not present at the reading and I told her so. There is something, that I will never do, and that is to invent something. If I see a spirit or an angel with the person that I am reading for, I will tell the client so. If not, I will not. In this case the spirit entity was not present until about the middle of the reading. I could tell that the entity was a woman and one that was older as she approached us form the world of spirit. It was her mother, and the daughter was happy to make the connection with her mother. At the end of the reading the matter the daughter had brought with her had been resolved to the satisfaction of both mother and daughter.

Not too long after I moved to Florida, a close friend and his wife called and asked Patricia and me to come down to their summer home in another part of Florida called Margate for a visit. Upon arriving, we spent most of the time just talking about old times and the hometown that we knew, and how things had changed. Even in a small town setting life has a way of moving on. As the day went on I had a feeling that the father of my friend was present in the house. The house was owned by his father and upon his passing was left to my friend. The subject of Steve's father came up, and he was very close to his dad. I mentioned that his father was with us today and was happy to be here. This was great for Steve, the fact that he always felt the presence of his dad with him. Perhaps this gave him confirmation that what he was sensing was his father and not his imagination.

Most of us today have problems of one kind or another, and when they become troublesome it is at these times that we will seek the advice of a Medium to shed some light on the issue at hand. When people with problems come to me for a reading, they find that my guide at times will become a little blunt with them because of my guide's insistence on relaying the truth. I know my guide well enough to realize that when she says something, she is saying it with a great deal of truth, and will not pull any punches to get the message across. It's good that people want the messages to be presented that way, with good old-fashioned honesty. In the church where I started my Mediumship, we had what was called 'Mediums Day.' The church was open to the public, and each of the Mediums would give a fifteen-minute reading to interested persons. After finishing up with several of the readings, I had one individual sit in front of me and ask for a reading. For some reason, something didn't feel right, but I started the reading anyway. This was the first time that I had drawn a blank. I couldn't even get a word from spirit. Nothing was coming through from my Spirit Guide to help this person, just a blank. I said to the person "I am not getting anything from my helpers, so can we just sit here and talk? I will give your money back" at this time his girlfriend came over and told me that no one could read for him, because he was very negative on this subject - so we just sat and talked. Perhaps that is what he needed in the first place and not a reading, just someone to take the time and listen to him.

The point is, that there are times when a Medium will come up short for one reason or another and it could be that the Medium and the person just do not connect. There are times that the person is just blocking the reading - in other words they really do not want to be read for. Whatever the reason, it doesn't happen too many times, but once is enough! This becomes a good test for the Medium. If your Spirit Guide is there, you can often get beyond this and surprise the person you are reading for. People still come to Mediums and express disbelief that there are no crystal balls or other objects that look like what they had seen in the movies. I assure you that true Mediums will only have their Spirit Guides with them, and that's all!

In another situation, a man came into the reading room I was using at a house party. He sat down and said, John, I don't believe in this. My wife-to-be twisted my arm to get me here." I said, "Okay, lets start anyway." After the reading he looked at me and said, "How *did you* do that". I told him that I wasn't doing the work - that my Spirit Guide was doing it, and that I am just a vehicle. I don't know if he fully understood that, but he asked me to officiate at their wedding later that year. There have been many nonbelievers that will come through the door of a Mediums office and leave as believers, marveling that the Medium knows that much about them. With all the readings I have done over the years, and the many nice letters that I have received, it not only makes me feel good, but also shows that there is a great need for more of the work to be done. Unfortunately, many people forget to tell the Medium how they truly feel after the readings. These are topics that some need to hear so they know where they stand with their Spirit Guides, and if they need any adjustments along the way. I have received letters and phone calls about my readings that make me feel confident to continue on with the work as a Medium and to encourage others to get involved in it. People's interest in Mediumship is on the rise, and there is a great need for good professional Mediums to carry on the work.

"WORDS FROM BEYOND"

I have found that when a spirit wants you to do something, whether it is Mediumship or writing other books, they will do everything they can to get your attention, from tapping you on the shoulder, to (as in my case) a swift kick you-know-where. It was that gentle kick from Gladys that prompted me to start this chapter "Words From Beyond", outlining the workings of spirit as told by the spirits in their own words. Much of the rest of this book comes from some of the guides that have been with me for years. They are assisting me in this new endeavor. In these chapters there will be different Spirit Helpers that will come through in order to add their support in the framework of the text, each having a great amount of information that they give out. I must admit there were times when I thought it was just me. I have many years of knowledge that had stuck in the old mind of mine. I sat at the computer, pushing out words on the keyboard, words at the time I was not too sure of. However, I found that it was not me. There was just no way that I could have the information that was coming out on the screen. During the process of writing this book I stayed away from other materials on the subject matter that could have an impact on our work. This helps me be sure the information is coming directly from the world of spirit and not from me, or something that I have read.

Part of the reason for writing this part of the book came from when I was attempting to finish up what I thought was going to be the last chapter. I let Pat, my better half; check the chapters to see if I made some errors in the spelling and sentence structures. She's good at looking at my work with an objective eye also; which is good for any writer. I remember it as if it was just the other night. I was at work and, as usual, would call her to see how things were at home. On this night, I also wanted to see if she had finished reviewing the last chapter. She mentioned to me the chapter was one that she could not put down and that I could not use it as the last chapter in the book.

As you might imagine, that did not go over too well with me at all. I was looking at myself becoming old and gray before this book would be ready to go. With her Cape Cod sense of humor she managed to calm me down long enough to explain to me what she had on her mind. She explained that the chapter was too good to be just a chapter in itself, but an outline for a book of messages from the spirit side - with the spirits using their own words. I thought of what a neat idea. People would be getting insight into the world that we know so little about in today's society, even from the halls of the religious institutions themselves. Perhaps with the support of my guides I would be able to obtain a key that would open the door to their world. Perhaps I could peek in and see how the residents live, along with what makes them want to add their support to our personal existence while we struggle through life. It is possible that with some added understanding we can better understand ourselves. Before I sat down with the idea of finishing this part of the book I had to ask my guides to help me in the necessary process of what to say, how to put it in the framework of written text, and still make some sense. I still had one major problem, one that I am sure that most writers think about from time to time when they start. Can I keep it within the way that spirit wants me to say it, and yet make it readable for my readers? With that in mind, I sat down with pen in hand - well computer, at my fingertips, and proceeded to pound out an outline of the subjects that I would ask my guides to answer in each chapter. I just had to keep myself open and ready to receive their information.

When I'm giving a reading, I personally like to receive information that get to the point of the matter but enough information to make them stop and think about the matter at hand. Knowing my guides the way that I do, I was sure that this would be the way it would pour out from them.

With this entire thought running around inside my head, I became more determined to do the best that I could with the book. Yet I had still some reservations on the material itself. I sat at the keyboard ready to proceed with the writing and yet with some hesitation, one of my guides decided to help.

Marion (one of my teachers) with her writing skills as a teacher came swishing in beside me telling me that she was about to take over the writing of this part of the book. She would include the topics that would be of interest to my readers along with some information that I was not aware of at the time.

I wasn't surprised that Marion would take over that way. She was a teacher while here on the Earth side – and one with control. For her to now be that interested in my work was a little surprising, but I was glad she was. Perhaps she felt that I was now ready to listen to what all my guides had to say.

I had done some writing in the past "Positive Affirmations To Live By" was one of my first books dealing with spiritualism. This book, however, would be a little different - in that it is a direct link with the world of Mediumship and Spirit and their actual input. Perhaps this was the reason why Marion had taken a greater interest in my work this time. When I reflect back, she always did show interest - even in the classes that I attended back in good old

Massachusetts, where she was one of the teachers in Mediumship Development. I remember Marion's personality. She was a strong woman and much like Gladys, was rarely silent for a lack of words. You either got along with her or you didn't. In a way, she was much like a nun in her teaching style. Although, once you allowed yourself to know her and her ways, you had a friend not only for life but also beyond. Since her passing, she is now home as I have come to realize. As you will note, Marion along with other helpers, offered to give me a great deal of information for the construction of the chapters in this book in the preparation for publication.

In the years that I have been involved in reading for people, I have found that there are many who are still looking for the right answers to some age old and yet unanswered questions. Perhaps this section of the book will offer some of those answers.

It is interesting that some of the world's religions don't want to tread in this territory of life on the other side of the veil. They believe that one part of the other side is called heaven, and is only for the ones that deserve to go there. The rest of it is a place that we do not want to even think about, and it is called hell. They believe it is pretty much where the journey of life takes us. Spiritualism teaches, however, that the world of spirit is not that far away place as one thinks. In fact it is adjacent to our own world. It also teaches us that there is no Heaven or Hell on the other side of life. It's right here on Earth. Hell is only the separation from God, and Heaven is the life you can have here on Earth if you choose.

The only thing that separates us from their world is what is called "rate of vibration". This is one of the workings of what is called "Natural Law", which governs the universe itself. It is interesting that we enter the spirit world each and every day without even knowing it. Perhaps even we are even walking through a room of the one that is now living on the other side.

Today we are living in a world that is one of exploration. We shoot a rocket into space and haven't hit God - leaving the question "Where is heaven in the first place"? People are not just accepting the words of others, but are now challenging ideas that we have been taught since birth. Perhaps it means throwing out the traditional teachings and philosophies, and adding a pinch of open-mindedness. I remember as a child stepping out a little and challenging authority when it came to religious matters and was looked at religion a little differently than the other children in the class. I am not sure if the teacher was having a problem with either getting me ready for the priesthood or just giving up on me, and my challenging of the ideals we were expected to believe. Later in life I found that people like me were also interested in obtaining the right answers on matters that were being overlooked or not being discussed in the forum of the public eye. Perhaps the time is "now", that humans and the world of spirit can work together in an attempt to bring some new light to the subject at hand. I don't know all the answers. I believe that no one here on the Earth truly does. There are many who receive glimpses of these things and place them to one side. With the help of my Spirit Guides and the ones that are supporting them, we will attempt to answer a few of these questions the best that we can.

One question of interest is spirit's concept of God. What does God appear to be like to those on the other side of life?

When you start communicating with your spirit guides, you will find that God is a little different to them than what we here perceive it to be. God is nothing like the pictures you see in books. The magnificence of God is in all that there is. God is neither female or male or animal. As they explain it God is visible in everything we see, and also invisible in all that we feel and sense. Another questions that always comes up is the one about loved ones who have passed into the spirit side of life -

whether they are okay, and do they still love the ones who are left behind? Something else I hear a lot is "I need to ask them for forgiveness for things that I said or did to them or to tell them things I wanted to say and never did."

Over the years people have mentioned to me that they feel the presence of one of their parents in their home. They ask me if this is their parents touching in from the spirit side of life. When I tell them that it is, they look at me with a sense of relief. Its as if a weight was just lifted off their shoulders. This is usually followed by the expression "Good, I am not crazy".

Here is something of interest. Some children in their early years see what is often called ghosts. They are also often thought of as their imaginary playmate. It is possible that these playmates are your child's guides who came with them to the Earth side. They're here to help the child make some adjustments with their new residence here on the Earth plane.

There are other questions that plague us from time to time - like "does each of us have what is called a blueprint of our lives that outlines before birth the events we will go through when we arrive here on the Earth"? If so, is this is called the "book of life?"

We, as you will find, do not come to the Earth unequipped - but with a great deal of information to help us navigate our way through this life. We come with at least one, perhaps more, assigned guides who work to assist us in the process. As you can see, we are ready for our Earth adventure. We arrive with the tools we need to survive here on this, our new home, tucked within the vastness and complexity of the universe.

When we witness the birth of a new baby, it appears to have (from all usual points of view) just dropped in. We forget the workings behind the scene of spirit before the infant arrived to its new home. The interesting thing is this process applies to all of God's creations from the birds to the trees. As you can imagine there is a special designer behind this complex arrangement of all that is available to us.

One of the curiosities that is now coming up is "do we have visitors here from the other side to help us in our march through life? Are these visitors like ones from the angelic world? If so, do they come in the way that we expect to perceive them or are they like you and I - someone who walks the streets ready to help us in time of need?"

It is more than possible that these angels are amongst us already, and in our daily existence. We see them and don't know who they are until we need them. The concept of wings has always bothered me. I believe they are not restricted in the world of spirit. They would have no need for wings as a means of movement. This is a world where movement is by means of thought. History, (like artist, churches) however, has expounded the opposite and has placed wings on them.

Another of today's concerns is the fear of the unknown and how to deal with it. With the events of Sept 11th and the loss of all those people at the World Trade Center, people are now looking into other means of understanding themselves and the world that they live in. Here again, the issue of life after death comes creeping through the minds of each of us.

In my religious pursuit, I often think about what happens to us in the after life we call heaven. Do we become closer to God and sit beside him, or are we cast into the fiery place to reside there forever? These are questions that have been thought about throughout time. Will we see our loved ones again once we arrive at the gates of heaven or not? We know about the so-called subdivision of the spirit world into the three places call heaven, hell and purgatory. These are places that had been taught by religious leaders for over hundreds of years.

Countless generations were told not to question whether these places exist or not.

One of the interesting items that has come up in the last few years is that now both heaven and hell are considered a state of consciousness and not a real place. This new, and yet old, understanding is a little Earth shaking to a lot of people including churches of all forms of religions.

One day I was talking to a minister from a different religion about the concept of heaven and hell. His answer was the traditional reaction - and that is "yes, one can be sent to hell if he or she does not believe in this or that." Upon hearing that remark, I asked him if he had children and they disobeyed him, what would he do to them? Would he hold them over the stove?"

He looked at me with a puzzled expression and said, "That is ridiculous."

I answered it is - if we have a merciful God I don't believe he would do that to us.

His only statement after that was "Will I see you at church this Sunday?"

I think you know my answer.

I must admit, I don't have all the answers, - not even some of the ones we would like to know. However I will attempt to explore as much as I can with the support of my guides. I'll do this with the intent of opening the doors just a little wider, so we can peer in to the world of spirit and learn some of their knowledge of both the Earth and their world.

The title of this chapter and those after it "Words From Beyond" was given to me by Marion, so the credit must go to her and some of the other Spirit Helpers that have taken the time to offer their in-depth information to these chapters ~~and the statements in it~~. I must admit that after all the years of Mediumship and doing readings for different people who have a variety of guides, I still come away with new understanding that makes me want to learn more. It also shows that we still have a lot more to understand about the other side and the way spirit works with us here.

I had a friend in high school named Jack. He and I were friends throughout our school years. He would always say "learn something new every day". That statement stuck in my mind over the years. He is right; we have to learn new things in order to grow in life and to extend our knowledge.

I believe that you could be in this work as a Medium for a number of years and still learn something new regarding spirit's function with us on the Earth side.

Every time I do a reading for someone, I stop and think about how each one differs from the last one. It's good that I don't remember any of them for more than a few seconds and how spirit seems to have all the right answers for the person that I'm reading. They manage to give the answer in a matter of seconds!

At these times I have asked myself "How do they do this and be accurate in the process?" I am what they call a rapid Medium, one who reads quite fast. Thanks to Gladys, my main guide, I have the means to read for a large group of people. I have done this so many times, both here and in New England. In doing so it is interesting to learn that a group of spirits will work together as a team to get the information out to the people without ego. We can learn a great deal from this method of sharing here on the Earth side.

I have learned that it takes a great amount of love in order for spirit to come to the Earth side. To them, our world is quite dark in comparison to their world. It is like going to a dark room in your home. That is how our Earth appears to them. When you turn on the light, the brightness is how their world is.

That means their love and support for us is very strong in order for them to enter the Earth's vibration to support a loved one who they left behind. That is one of the reasons we receive some of their vision from time to time and just let it go with out thinking about it. We can and should learn a lot of interesting things from them so we can live a better existence while on the Earth as we travel through life's ups and downs.

As I have mentioned before, each of us has at least one, perhaps more, guides who stay with us from birth until we are ready to go home to the spirit side. I have a guide named Brother Francis - a monk who I have been with in a different century. He has been with me before birth and remains with me to this day.

Marion is one of my helpers who has taken the liberty of helping me with this book. I knew Marion as one of my teacher in Mediumship work and she was one that was a terrific person.

There are others entities who also have given me information to relay and I will mention them as we move on in the chapters. Each one has given me the necessary information and added their love in the message. I asked them one day why I started late in life doing this work and their answer was; "You were not ready at the time." Perhaps I was not.

"SPIRIT PERCEPTION OF GOD"

How does the other side see God? Do they see this God as we do here on the Earth side or do they have a different perception of God? Even today, there is a question whether there is a God or not. So where is this God when you need him - when the time of need comes knocking at my door?"

There is no doubt in my mind that there is a God and that God is in everything we see within the universe. However, it is still good to receive confirmation from our spirit friends on the subject. In my dealings with spirit I have found that, first and foremost, there is a God who is present within the universe and beyond, the entity that we usually think of when someone mentions God. Does God look like us? I hope not! Where does this God live? In a heaven that is far away or right within oneself? Many of us were taught what to believe as children - perhaps by nuns and priests who would make us learn the definition. To this day, I can still remember the definition that was drilled into me. It goes like this "God is the creator of both heaven and Earth and all things." That definition is right out of the little blue book called "The Baltimore Catechism", a book we, as Catholic kids, had to use in order to learn all about God and what he has done for us. The book became our bible and part of our religious lives. We were compelled to learn these pages by heart or find ourselves sitting there writing them out until our fingers became numb. I believe that was one of the ways I learned it - reciting them to the priests who stood in front of me with the face of sternness about them. Good heavens. If we didn't know them by the end of the day, the priests would reveal the true concept of hell to us!

When you stop and think about it that was a tough way of indoctrinating the youth into the understanding of God and the religion that they were in. I believe that this has changed a little today, and now the students of religion are receiving a different concept. Back then, in my youth, it was quite different. The old method left a bad taste for a long time, and many of us over the years had second thoughts regarding the concept of religion. Once out of the classes, many completely stopped going to church. The priests taught that if we were resentful of God, we were in for some trouble - so we had a great deal of respect or perhaps fear of the God who we came to know. We came away with the perception that God was way up in the sky, sitting on a golden throne and passing out judgments to all that entered his domain. It was as if sinful people were set to one side of the room for a trip to a fiery place, the good ones just were accepted in heaven, and the balance would be placed in some other place for future consecration.

In my studies of the history of religion, I found the concept of God varies in many ways. Only one thought that remains constant - that there is a God (or a source that is called God) who created the whole works we call Earth.

In this book, I have taken the position of asking one of my guides to help me to understand how they see God from their eyes and how this view of God relates to our view here on the Earth. My concept of God is that of a merciful God, but one who doesn't immediately step in when someone starts messing up life. Is this how we end up with the many wars and persecution that has mankind plagued?

It would seem that people today have a hard time understanding God altogether in the changing world we live in. At one extreme, there are those who will say there is no God at all. Their logic says, "How could there be a God that would allow so much disruption to the world?" they believe it's only the people who determine their fate.

Every time we turn on the radio or television, we are confronted with some form of disaster that makes us stop and wonder "what is next?" When we see people living on the streets

- not only in other countries, but in our own as well - should we start blaming God for their position in life? Personally, I have a hard time placing the blame on God. Perhaps there are other reasons why these things happen. I believe in a God-power and this power is that of a master builder who has put it all together for us, for both things that are seen and that which just now we are beginning to see.

A good friend of mine is a Minister of a different faith. He is what is called a Humanist. He's one who must have it proven to him that God does exist before he'll believe. As you may be able to guess, we have had some very interesting discussions over the matter. Although our ideas are quite different, we've remained friends over the years. I still have the hope that he will in time learn that God does exist and he is a part of this wonderful power. We used to go to lunch from time to time, and it was on one of these occasions that I remember the minister shut the car door on his foot.

Without thinking, he said "oh God", and I turned to him and said, "I told you so"!

However, there are still some people who will argue that from a scientific standpoint everything was started from the big bang and that there is no God at all.

With the advent of September Eleventh, many people that perhaps were on the line with their faith made an effort to come back to the faith they grew up with. Perhaps they feel that by going back into their churches that they *wish* event will go away?

One of my helpers that who has been assisting me with this book is Pauline. I knew her in life as a fellow student at the Onset Church in Onset Massachusetts. There, we were groomed to become Mediums, and later worked together at many of the church functions, like sitting for mini-readings that the church offered once a month. Pauline passed into the spirit side of life at an early age and was deeply missed by all who knew her.

Some time later she came to me as one of my assistant helpers and remains with me to this day. In fact, she used to call me Brother John - and still does from her new home in spirit.

In this part I will open it up with asking Pauline about how she understands God from the other side of life. The intent is not to upset your faith but to perhaps open up your mind to another way of thinking. This is what Pauline had to say about her idea of God as viewed from the spirit side of life.

J: Pauline, one of the questions that I must ask is "do you see God the way that we do here on the earth side"?

P: No, not that way.

J: Then how do you see God?

P: The God that you on Earth have in mind is one of form and texture with a pinch of Shape to it. That concept is incorrect in all ways.

J: We can only perceive God the way it was taught to us. Each of us perceives God the way we have been taught in some form of religious training or through resource materials that we study.

P: So? That is still incorrect.

J: Then please explain to us what God looks like.

P: Before we go into that let me tell you that we call your God the source.

J: Well I can personally accept that, and I think others will agree.

P: God is not one to be bowed down to, like your
Earth expects. The source created each of us to enjoy life and come into contact to the source for support - not to be placed upon the throne or worshiped.

J: You know, Pauline that is the type of God I would want to know better. The idea of a source makes more sense to some of us seeing where the word "source" means to be the original starting point of the whole thing. The Old Testament makes God appear to be quite

P: You've done well, for that is what the source is truly like.

J: Some people believe there are many definitions of God. Is that true?

P: Yes, there is much to the source you call God.

J: Then we can say that God is a spirit?

P: No, that is only in your understanding.

J: Then if God is not a spirit, what is God?

P: First it would be hard for Earth people to give a definition of God because it cannot be done.

J: How are we to understand what God truly is?

P: That is the hard part - your attempt to understand.

J: Why is that?

P: You are basically still human. I can remember talking to a man and the topic of God came up, he mentioned that he did not truly believe in God for he could not touch, see or feel this God, so therefore God does not exist. That is interesting statement in that most people feel the same way, that in order to understand something you must ether see it or at least touch it.

J: Well there must be some part of us that accepts the concept of God.

P: Yes. Your soul does.

J: Then our soul knows the true God better than the human part of us?
P: That is correct.
J: Prior to writing this book my guide, Brother Frances, had been gently hinting to me about the function of our soul and the vast knowledge that is contained in it. I thought it was very interesting when he mentioned that if we need to obtain this information, we could do so. That in the soul itself is the link to who and what God is truly all about.
P: Your soul knows, however your mind cannot comprehend the concept.
J: Then our mind and soul are different?
P: No, your soul is also part of the mind. Your mind stays with you but your thought processes go with the soul.
J: Okay. I think I understand what you are talking about.
P: Your soul does and that is good enough.
J: You mention that it would be hard for us here on Earth to place a definite image of God?
P: It would be impossible.
J: Okay, you see this God as a source. How does this source appear to you from the other side? Perhaps
we can get some understanding of how to see this source.

P: Our perspective of the source is one of a bright light of many colors that emanate from it.
J: Does this source have any form to it?
P: No.
J: You mention that the source has colors to it. What types of colors does the source have?
P: There are ones that you see Earth side like blues, pinks and others. Then there are many more that you cannot conceive.
J: Does the source have any size to it?
P: When we see the source it could. At other times it varies in sizes and colors.
J: Does the source speak to you and others over there?
P: No, not the way you speak to others. It is more mental.
J: So the communication between you and the source is one that is not audible but more of thought?
P: Yes, that is how each of us hears the source when information is given.
J: What type of information is given by the source?
P: Answers to whatever we want to know.
J: So you can talk on any subject that you need to know about?
P: Yes.
J: Is there any personality connected to the source?

P: There is just pure love, not a drop of anger or hostility for any one or thing.

It would appear that Pauline is talking about a loving God, one that most of us here on the Earth side expect and that goes a little against the judgment form of God that was taught us in our youth.

J: Why do we here on the Earth side have a hard time tuning into the source for help?
P: Each one of you can, and some do - but your mind wants an image of something that is not there.
P: Each Earth soul will tap into the source and enjoy the visit but their minds will grab onto old images and the process is again lost.
J: What would be the best way to tune into the source?
P: Just accept.

The answer that Pauline just gave about accepting was one that I had to explore. I am not too sure if she was talking about the inner feeling that each of us has from time to time or the way books outline God?

J: Pauline you mention about accepting God or the source, and I would like to know how we here go about this?

P: Brother John, acceptance is a knowing that the source is just there and you can receive a glimpse of the source each day as you observe the light of the Earth.

J: There are people on the Earth side that truly want to know their God better.

P: That is true, however some of them still allow their mind to run their lives, let alone allow themselves to see the real source. Here again, it is hard to change our concept of God from the way we have been taught over the years. Once it is placed in our minds the teaching of what God appears to be, makes it hard to imagine it could be something different. To attempt to perceive God as a source or light that is just there is not easy for some, however if that is the way it is seen from the other side. Perhaps we should take another look at this concept.

J: Does the source have a so-called kingdom as indicated by most religions?

P: There is no such kingdom, the source is everywhere in everything, all at one time. The idea of there being no kingdom is one that is now coming out from the Vatican in Rome. It's a big step for the followers of that faith to come to grips with - after all these years. Perhaps this is a break through for what is to come.

J: Pauline, when the source is talking to you or to others, where do you go? Is there a special place, like a church?

P: Wherever we want. The source is everywhere. You can worship God anywhere you want - including the beach. God is not restricted to be only in the houses of worship.

J: Does the source perform judgment upon us as we have been taught?

P: No you do that yourself.

J: So there is no fiery pit to roast in, if we committed a sin?

P: As I have mentioned, the source is one of great love not one of judgments.

J: So where does this leave sin?

P: Right where it started. It's just a word. That's not to say that we can go out and commit offenses against people and feel that the source will not look at you with a little remorse, but it is a fact that the one making the offense will become remorseful himself.

J: I can see why it can become difficult to define and understand this God.

P: I told you that. People of your world have this perception of their God and it won't fly in our eyes.

J: Pauline, your concept of our God may not fly over here?

P: That's not quite true, there are many people who need a better insight of God than they have been taught on your world.

J: I feel that is quite true.

P: No one will be left out of this understanding. That is not the source's way.
J: Pauline, does the source summon you to go to it?
P: No, I just go where I want.
J: So, as you have already mentioned, there is no particular place that you and others go to?
P: No. There is no particular place or church that we go to. If we elect to go by the sea or the mountain, it's up to us.
J: When you arrive at the place do you pray or just talk to the source?
P: No there is no need for prayer. Brother John,
J:I believe we here on Earth fear God in a way.
P:That is so wrong. That is because in our history o
J:There seems to be some struggling because of the priest situation. As of this writing the Church has been having problems with their priests and children that have been coming forward.
P: Ha! Struggling is not the right word. That will become the last straw for many religions.
J: We need religion to find God.
P: No, you need yourself to find the source.
J If that is true, what will happen to religion?
P: The answer to that question is - look at it now.
J: You sound a little bitter about religion.

P: No not bitter, just disappointed.

J: In what way?

P: Just look at the action of its history, and how it has caused problems today.

J: Again each of us still needs something.

P: Yes, you need to be there - where each will find the source.

J: Why won't the source come on to the Earth and help to pull it together?

P: Why should it?

J: Because we here need the help.

P: The source did not create the mess. Man did. It is up to mankind to work together to do this.

J: I don't think we can.

P: You are so right.

J: So we in large numbers should pray for peace?

P: You need to do much more. You need to work in peace in order to obtain it the way it should be.

J: I guess we have our work cut out for us.

P: Work in peace and harmony and the world will be much better.

J: Is this what happened to Atlantis?

P: Yes and the planet Mars.

J: I have always had this liking for Mars.

P: There are many reasons for that.

J: We can get into that later.

P: Fine.

J: Pauline is the source male or female?

P: Neither.

J: So it is both?

P: Source does not need a gender to create, you do.

J: I was under the impression that the source, or God, was a combination of both.

P: No, the source does not need to be.

J: I must ask your view on the trinity.

P: What about the trinity?

J: Are there three different parts of God or the source?

P: You mean the father, son and spirit?

J: Yes.

P: No, there are many denominations, or segments, of the source - but not the three you just mentioned.

J: But the source has several faces?

P: It can have millions of faces if it wants to. In fact each of the Earth people are part of the many faces of your God.

J: That is because we

P: Yes we are all connected.

J: We could be the many faces of God that is mentioned?

P: Yes. Each of us both in your world and others are all connected.

J You mentioned earlier that our soul can relate to the source in a way which we can understand the source. Is that all facets of the source?

P: Yes, your soul never forgets anything.

J: So, we, even in this human form, have some attraction to the source?

P: Yes.

J: Does that mean that we can just talk to the source as if we were talking to a friend?

P: That is the idea.

J: It makes the dialog with the source more on a personal basis.

P: That's the way it was ment to be.

J: Pauline, it's good that you have placed this on a simple basis and not a complicated one.

P: There is no need for that. Life on your world is complicated enough.

J: That is for sure.

P: Life on Earth must be enjoyed and lived each day as if it was your last.

J: That is a great concept.

P: It is the only way. Look what happened to me. One of the ways to live on your world is to use balance in all that you do. I passed into spirit at a young age and was as alive then as I am now over here. My statement of balance of life while on the Earth side is very important and is one that we must remember each day.

J: Is that what the source wants?

P: Yes. Perfect balance brings perfect existence.

J: That makes a great deal of sense. Pauline does the source enter all churches?

P: Sure. That's where a great many people meet.

J: That is true. Does the source have any comments on religion, as we know it?

P: No, the source accepts all, if the heart is the main purpose.

J: Pauline, I want to thank you for your insights and support in this part of the book about your concept of God. It is good to have a different perspective on this.

"THE WORLD OF SPIRIT"

It was called the Summerland in the century past. We now call it the spirit world. However we refer to it, the state does exist. It's a wondrous place, from what I have been told, and the ones that come from there are not only interesting, but also helpful to us here on this place we call (for a time) home. However we look at it, the spirit world and its workings are not easy to understand, let alone explain to others who are interested in learning.

As I continue to write this book, it is Marion's turn to come back to me. Which is just fine with me.

What Marion said to me was "let's talk about things that apply to us over here in the world of spirit, as you refer to it."

I thought that it would be a great idea, seeing that I never took the time to sit down and ask any of my guides in depth about their new home. The exploration of this world from the viewpoint of spirit will give us a new way of looking at it and give us a new understanding of the working of this world behind the veil.

There have been books written on the subject of the after life as far back as the Egyptian period. They prepared themselves for the journey back to the other side and their new life in the world of spirit. This sounds like they must have had some knowledge of the topic.

Like most of us growing up the idea of an after life seemed like something that was out of the realm of understanding. It's one that was not discussed much, perhaps out of fear of the unknown.

It would appear that the subject was out of the realm of knowledge for our religious teachers, for all that was mentioned was the fact that we go to heaven and sit beside God.

When my father passed into spirit at a young age, even with the belief I had, it still was hard for me to understand the whole concept of what happens to the soul after death. Where do we really go? Is it possible that we do appear before God and receive some form of judgment for our deeds and get sent to one place or other? Or does the other side resemble this side in some respect? One of the questions that is asked a lot: "What happens when we arrive on the other side?"

There were many questions to be answered, so I sat quietly at the computer to put this chapter together with the help of Marion to answer some of these questions. In doing so, my mind would drift back to my childhood days and the teaching that I acquired. Marion started opening the doors to a whole new understanding. This new understanding was astonishing and was contradictory to what had taught.

J: Marion, could you give us some look at the world that you are in now?
M: What would like to know first?
J: I would like to know is how far the other side is from where we are on the Earth?
M: There are many levels to the other side and the first level is quite close to the material world.
J: I remember you talking about the many levels that exist in your world.
M: That is right. There are more levels that can be counted.
J: Does each level represent different concepts of the other side?
M: Sure, each level has different properties.
J: So when we refer to the other side, are we talking about one level of the other side?
M: A fraction of the other side.
J: Could you give us some idea of what you mean by these levels?
M: Yes. There are many levels, and as one progresses here, they move to a new level
J: These levels - are they levels to new understanding?
M: Yes. As one comes here, one will, in time, learn new things and these levels that one

goes through- will help to acquire this new understanding.

J: Do these levels mean that if a person is on a higher one, they are smarter?

M: No, we don't have that here. Each one is looked at as the same.

J: Now tell me about your side of life. Is it like the Earth side?

M: The first level is like the Earth, with all the amenities that your world has.

In some of the old books on spirit communication that I have read, the concept of what the other side on the first level looks like is much like the Earth itself. Some that have passed into the other side believe that they are still Earth bound.

J: Does the other side have homes and buildings, like the ones we have?

M: Yes. Let me tell a little more about what is here, as one comes here.

J: what is this tunnel?

M: It is the path to here. When one arrives, they are amazed at the similarity of their new world to that of Earth. In fact some think they have never left the Earth.

J: It must be a shock when someone tells them they did.

M: This does not happen right off. We work with them, so that in time, they will adjust to where they are.

J: To them t is like their home and surroundings?

M: That is correct. There is a great deal of love here and our job is to help them to feel at home.

J: Then after that, what happens?

M: Don't get ahead of me.

J: Okay.

M: There is beauty of many colors here and it is hard for you who live on the Earth to understand.

J: As you know, I have read books on it. So I have some understanding.

M: Your books don't do it justice. As we have told you some time ago, the ponds are abundant and the seas are now full of life, unlike the ones on your world.

J: One of the books that I read mentions that the trees and flowers are of such beauty that the colors stand out as if lights were coming from them.

M: That is quite true.

J: What types of buildings are there?

M: All types - whatever you want to have.

J: Does that mean that we create our own buildings over there?

M: Just like you do in your world. Let me go on and tell you more about this side.

J: That sounds good to me.

M: There are so many different subjects to talk about that it could take all day. The fact is that all who enter this side are well taken care of. They need time to adjust; we work with them so that they can. We have what you may call hospitals, so that the new arrivals will be looked after. We call this a way station. These way stations are places where the new arrivals spend some time adjusting to their new environment and learn what they can and cannot do. Way stations have a great deal of support from many of the ones who have been there over the years.

J: Does the adjustment to your new world depend on the persons understanding before they came to your world? If one has this preconceived notion about what the other side is like and base that idea on what was passed to them by their religions - upon arrival I guess they will have to make some drastic changes.

M: Yes, that has a large part to play with the adjustment time.

J: Is it true that if we learn about your world while we're here, when we arrive, it will become easy to adjust?

M: Yes, if you wanted to travel to England, you would look up the different places that you wanted to go and plot the direction to get there. Before you come here, you should study the area the best way you can.

J: Is that one of the reason why we go to your world some times at night? Over the years, I have been told that we travel in our sleep at night to the other side and upon waking we don't remember a thing. This traveling to the other side is not lost for it is imbedded in the soul for future use.

M: Yes. There is some that, once they come back to your world, refuse to understand - so upon their arrival we have to re-educate them over again.

J: It sounds like each of you has different assignments.

M: Yes we just don't sit around all day.

J: What else do you do?

M: My job is to help others make the transition to this side.

J: It sounds as if you spend time at these way stations helping the new arrivals to make the necessary adjustments to their new place.

M: Others have their functions that are assigned to them.

J: Who makes the assignments?

M: We have what is called a council that works with the assignments.

J: I would think that the source would make the assignments.

M: No, the source is the overseer of all things.

J: So that is why I have seen a member of the council at times.

M: Yes.

J: How many are on the council?

M: There are twelve.

J: That number keeps coming up, is there a reason?
M: Yes!
J: Marion, you mention that the council makes assignments, could you explain exactly what they do?
M: Well, they help the new arrivals as they come in from your world. They also assign a guide to the ones who are going to the Earth side.
J: How many guides does each one have?
M: You have one main guide that is with you at all time and others that will assist in time of need.

Since the time of this writing, I have found that perhaps there is more than one guide who comes to the Earth plain with us. Perhaps we have many that support us while here. This is one of the questions that I had to ask Marion to explain.

J: Each of us could have more than one Spirit Guide?
M: Sure. In times of need you could have a group with you - all helping.
J: And this is all arranged at the council level?
M: Yes.
J: Marion, could you tell me just now many guides each of us would have?
M: More than one.

J: I was under the impression that we each had only one who comes with us and stays with us until we head back?

M: See, you still can learn.

J: Yes, and that surprises me.

M: It just shows that you have a great deal to learn about us here.

J: Yes.

At this point, I decided to change the subject and talk about something else. I know that I could have been on this subject for some time and I wanted to get to other matters of interest.

J: Would you tell me about the so-called Hall of Records? Where is it, or does it exist at all?

M: The Halls of Records are right there in you and there are times when you reflect upon them even on the Earth side. You call them memories.

J: There have been books written that mention about a Hall on the other side. It is a place where people go to review the lives they lived while on the Earth side. Is this true?

M: We do have places where people can go and reflect on matters of their life, yes.

J: Is one judged on what they have done on the Earth?

M: No. You judge yourself upon what you have done both on the Earth and on this side. Let me mention at this point that life here is a great deal like the life that each of you will go through on the Earth until one moves onto other levels, as I mentioned early in the text of your book.

J: I know that you were an animal lover. What happens to our pets when they go to the other side?

M: Animals are very special and are taken care of, with great care once here.

J: Do they go through the same process that we do before coming to the Earth?

M: We take the time to help them with their transition here, just as we do to each of you.

J: They are provided for then with lots of love?

M: Quite well.

J: What happens to things like trees that are here and decay?

M: They enter here, just like everything else. Nothing is ever wasted. As you can see, there is great care for everything that enters the Earth plane not just us in human form. In my teaching I have been taught about Natural Law and how it applies to all things including what is called nonliving things like trees and rock and they to have a rate of vibration attached to them.

J: If a person was a minister on this side of life or other profession, will they do the same thing there?

M: At first, yes. The individual will take on the same function as on the Earth side.

J: Do they change?

M: Yes, once they understand that there is no need to be so.

J: I have read there are colleges and universities of learning in your world. Is that true?

M: One can, and many do, go back to schools of higher learning.

J: Will these studies have anything to do with moving on to higher levels?

M: No. The source that will move you to higher levels is you and your willingness to learn what the source wants you to learn.

J: What would be some of these things that we need to learn? This seems to be the theme of all learning, here on the Earth side in religious teaching but never applied in true life.

M: Learning to love one other and to understand the laws of the universe.

J: That seems like a simple lesson to learn.

M: A simple lesson but difficult to do.

J: Why is it so difficult to do here on the Earth?

M: Being human is not easy, it is the ego that gets in the way and there lies the problem. Some mention that the ego is like another part of ourselves and tends to pulls us in a different direction in our lives.

J: How do we get rid of it so we can live in peace?

M: That is up to each of you who inhabit the Earth right now. There are a great number of issues that plague the world, and most of them are based on pride.

J: So the idea of loving each other is out?

M: If it is what the people of your world want, yes. However, that can, and must be, changed so that peace will follow.

J: Most of the world wants peace.

M: Yes, but at what cost?

J: Good point.

M: Each religion of your world must unite in prayer and ask for world peace.

That was the end of the day's work, it was not until the next day that I once again sat down at the keyboard of my slow moving computer and asked Marion for her help with the next part of the chapter.

The following is what became the next open session to a new understanding of how the soul is sent to the Earth side and cared for upon arrival to its new home.

It is amazing to look upon the birth of a new child and to see that old but new face of birth. One can only wonder the preparation that is required before a new arrival makes its way to our planet. When we as new parents see our first child we are amazed at the new life before us. It is one of the most remarkable events that can ever happen to a family, and all that matters is the care of the new little person with the big smile.

I remember calling my mother-in-law when our first was born. I said to her "its a boy and its twenty one feet long." There was a pause on the line as if it was disconnected and a voice came back saying, " what do you have up there?" I had to rethink what I'd said and then told her that it was still a boy, but he was twenty-one inches long.

As new parents we become quite excited at the event and it is like walking in a slight daze. It's as if you were the only one in the world that has gone through the process of being a father or mother. It was one of the happiest days of our life.

What occurs in the world of spirit when a new child is born? As the new baby makes the journey to the Earth, are they assigned a helper or guide or do they come alone? Does the new soul know what he or she is able to accomplish before traveling to the Earth plane? I put some of these questions to Marion with all the understanding that she has for us. This is what I asked Marion a few days later about what happens to the new arrivals to the Earth plane.

J: Marion I would like to ask you about the preparation for the new arrivals to our world.
M: Well, what do you want to know?
J: Before a new arrival makes the journey, what transpires?
M: There are a great many things that must first happen before we allow a new spirit to go back to your world.
J: Who makes the decision?
M: The council members.
J: It appears that this council makes a lot of the decision on these matters.
M: Yes, they have their hands full with all the different jobs that must be done.
J: Does a spirit go before the council for a request to come here to the Earth?
M: Yes, and it can be either accepted or rejected.
J: The council has the power to do so?
M: It is not a matter of power. It is the council's love, and knowing the outline of the request that has a bearing on the matter.
J: It sounds like it
M: No, and in fact there are times when a request is denied.
J: The council really takes a great interest in the spirit who comes before them.
M: Love is very strong here, and we want only the best for all - whether here or in your world.
J: That is nice! And I wish we all could live in peace and love.

M: The world can, and it must in order to survive.

J: When a spirit goes before the council to ask to for permission to go to the Earth plane, does the council pick their parents and location?

M: Yes, and it is up to the council to review their request at that time. The spirit will, if the council accepts the request, ask for a journeyer of their choice to go back with them. A journeyer is a Spirit Guide. All of us have one. This guide will stay with us until we go back to the spirit world, our old home. This Spirit Guide is one who will help us on our march through life on the Earth plane.

J: The spirits have the right to select their journeyer, or what we call a Spirit Guide, to come to the Earth side before birth?

M: That is correct, and it is up to the council will either approve the request or not. You must remember that the council makes these decisions for the benefit of the one going back.

J: But we do not come back alone?

M: No. One may have more then one guide with them as they enter the Earth plane.

J: It is mapped out for the new arrival?

M: Yes, down to the smallest detail.

J: Now Marion, what happens with the loss of a child at birth?

M: Before the new arrival enters the Earth, they can change their mind. At that time they come back to the world of spirit.
J: Does this happen a lot of times? Mothers will feel they' re the ones who caused the loss of their child, and for years blame themselves.
M: Yes, we know. We here feel the pain of the loss, as well as the mother does. However, remember that the child has the right, for one reason or another, to return. That is their choice to make.

In one of the readings I did, a woman came in with one question - to ask why she lost her child. This is very devastating to both parents and there is a feeling that perhaps one of them was the cause of the loss. My guide, Gladys said that it was the child in this case that made the decision to go back to the world it left. It was not the fault of either parent. As I passed this message that to the mother, I could see the relief that came over her. I learned a great deal myself that day about the decision that a soul has before and on the Earth side. Her husband, a non-believer, came in next for his reading with a little different attitude about what I explained to his wife. Both left with a good feeling.

J: Marion, there are people who would like to know their guides better. How can they go about contacting them?

M: The name of the helper is not important, but if they still want to know and can not figure it out for themselves, they could go to a good Medium and find out who their guide is. This may help them communicate with them on their own later.
J: We also have what I call helpers that are with us. Could you explain the working of these helpers?
M: The role of the helper is to assist the person in their growth in life and will stay with them until they have reached a desired level. At that time, they will leave and a new helper will come in and work with them on reaching the next level.
J: The helper is not assigned to you - but becomes attached to you when needed.
M: Yes. Attached may not be the word. They will come to a person in the time of need, as I mentioned before and then leave. This is one of the reasons a person will feel a shiver around them for a few days and then it will leave. This is the helper coming and going.
J: I was told that Gladys is not my guide at the time but elected to stay with me as for as long as I want. Can a helper receive permission from the council to stay with a person that long?
M: Yes, if the council thinks after hearing the request from the helper wish to remain with the person, the council can and - in your

case did allow it. We do all this with love and the understanding to help the one in need.

J: It is true that the council can, and sometimes will, deny the request of the spirit to stay?

M: Yes, it again depends on the needs and the plans of both.

J: There must be a plan or blue print of each person's life that is given to each of them before coming here. Is that right?

M:Yes, in a way. However, you have a right to make

J: If we don't live up the plan, does that mean we must come back to finish it up?

M:No. You are talking about karma? If you don't fin

J: We don't need to finish what we went Earth side for?

M: That is correct. Again, you have a choice.

J: If we do not finish what we went to the Earth side for, how will it affect us?

M:Well, you won't have to go back, however, you will still carry some of it when you do desire to travel back to the Earth side.

J: But we won't get struck in what we call a karmic debt?

M:No, not at all.

J: That's good to know. Most still believe that we must pay.

M:Not unless you want to. If there is true love, as we have here, then there is no need to make someone repeat these things or to have punishment imposed upon them.

J: I believe that most of us still believe in that though.

M: We have a loving source and that's important to bear in mind at all times.

J: Again will religions change their ways?

M: No.

J: Then there will still be this separation between religions of the world?

M: Yes, and that is the way it will be.

J: What about the ways we perceive God, will that chance?

M: To some, yes, to others, no.

"WORKING WITH SPIRIT GUIDES"

As a Medium working with spirits over the years, I have become quite amazed at the amount of information they offer and the love that goes with it. Over the twenty or so years I have, through the assistance of my guide, managed to help people that are in need from the very simple problems to the ones that need the support of what I call "heavy artillery".

In all this time, I maintain my commitment to present spirits actual words in readings to others when the need arises. At times it may be as small as "where is my lost cat that snuck out the door of my house" to ones having some severe marital problems. It comes in all forms.

I admit that when it comes to me, the task is a little more complicated and I have a hard time to just stop and listen to my own guides and get a kick from them in the process. With all that, they are still loyal to me and my work as a Medium, thank heavens! When you work with your Spirit Guide, you have to remember that these guides work with other spirit helpers as a team on their side in order to present the necessary information. The following conversation shows us some of what these guides go through in order to assist us here on the Earth side.

J: Marion, it is good to have you back today helping in my exploration.

M: It is good to be back and assisting you in your understanding of the workings of spirit.

J: Mediumship is not only interesting, but it helps so many on the path of life. Can you tell me a little about the workings of a Medium?

M: Well, first of all there needs to be two persons, one of the people doing the Mediumship and the working of the one over here that is willing to assist. Once the two come together, then and only then, will the process work?

J: I was under the impression that we are all Mediums.

M: That is correct, however, the ones that are willing to go forward with love will shine.

J: What happens to the ones that do not use their Mediumship?

M: It will not go to waste. They can use it in a different way, or perhaps pick it up later. Nothing is ever wasted.

J: When a Medium receives a message from spirit, is that spirit smart and have all knowledge about that person?

M: Not quite, it is not that easy to do. In the first place there is usually a group of other Spirit Helpers beside the one who is the significant one giving the message. The others will give their information when needed in the reading.

J: If there is a question about, oh, let's say someone's health issues, the main spirit might not have the answer, but would turn to the one that is equipped with that information, is that right?

M: Yes. You would not ask a builder to give a comment on teaching in elementary school.

J: I see what you mean. At times the answers still come quite fast

M: Not all the time. It depends on the Medium and the guide. There are some Mediums who are called "Rapid Mediums". They receive the message from spirit at a fast pace and relay that information quickly to their client.

J: When a person wants a reading, does the spirit drop what they' re doing, and go to the aid of the one helping the Medium?

M: Not quite.

J: Could you explain please?

M: Well, in a reading, the support group that is here will rally around the guide who is working with the Medium and participate in the reading. At times, there will be a line of helpers with the Medium in the attempt to help with the messages.

J: So this is a team effort.

M: Yes. We work together to help the ones over there and here.

J: Marion, do you think that the need for Mediums is coming back?

M: It really never left. The Earth people like to know what is in store for them and where they can go in their lives to better themselves.

J: I have found that more people are coming to me for readings in order to contact their loved ones who are now in spirit.

M: The contacting of the world of spirit has been going on for a long time and the connection with ones loved one is important for both, the one who is left behind and the one who is here in the world of spirit.

J: You know you brought up a point that I never thought too much about - and that is those in the world of spirit needing to contact those here in the material world.

M: Well sure. Don't you think we have some feeling about the world we lived in for all those years, and the people who we have been with, like you and others? When we see someone go on the wrong path we gather together in an effort to pull them back. When you are sad, we are sad. And we work hard to support you in your joys.

J: I never gave that part much thought.

M: We understand that living on the Earth is not fun. Everyone has their own problems that to them are massive in nature. We do understand. Many times helpers have been sent to your world to help but the person does not accept the help or do not believe that we have been back to help.

J: So you do keep your feelings when you pass over to the other side?

M: Well sure, but our feelings are different than yours. They're more intense and not for some but for all. You know that each of us here keeps our own individuality.

J: Yes, I was taught that also.

M: You know John; we are not what you call dead. We are very much alive.

J: That is what I have been told by my guides. On many occasions my guides have informed me they are very much alive - at times more so than we who reside here on the Earth. It may be hard to believe however, when you stop and think about it. Here on the Earth, we go through so much in order to just survive, where on the other side that is not the problem. That brings up a good question and it is "how do the ones in the world of spirit see us?

M: Do you really want to know?

J: Yes. Do you see us as we see ourselves, or as something different?

M: No, I am just kidding with you.

J: Good that makes me feel a little better.

M: Well, to us you look like lights that are in different places, some being very bright and others quite dim.

J: We are known as lights without form?

M: No. We see you as lights and are attracted to you because of it.

J: Each of us here have beacons of light that is known by each of you in spirit, is that correct?
M: That is almost right.
J: Well could you explain to me how that works?
M: When each of you arrived on the Earth side your soul is attached to you and it is called the aura. Those lights distinguish your soul
J: That is how you come to the ones that are in need?
M: Sure. It's just like a lighthouse with its beacon pointing the direction.
J: Why don't you see us as we truly appear?
M: We see the soul part of you, not the body that you have. It is the soul lights that help us find you.
J: That is how we appear to you?
M: Remember, you are spirit and a true spirit has no form. Your form is one of the Earths. When we arrive on the Earth side, we take on what is called a physical body so that we can move within the matter of the material world in which we now reside. However, the true self is the spiritual matter that is not seen by the naked eyes of humans. In the world of spirit we do not need the physical, but only the body of spirit in order to move about.
J: Do we take on different forms as we travel to higher levels over there?

M: No, the spirit form is one that will go on to each level. The form that you have on the Earth side is the one that you elected. It has become known to me that we on the other side elect a lot of things that we take for granted and one of them is the body that we feel would be to our advantage on Earth existence. Our parents are also the ones who we have chosen when we come to the Earth, along with the things that we must do in order to grow. The thing you have to remember is at night when you come over here, you come with the spirit form not the one that you are currently occupying.

J: Okay, that makes sense.

The statement that Marion made about coming over at night is one that I have heard over the year's - that the soul travels into the other world and we are then reeducated.

J: You mentioned that we travel to your side. Do we do that each night?

M: That depends on your sleep patterns and ones desire. People should understand that they can come over here at will.

J: I was under the impression that we go back at night to learn?

M: Yes, if you want to learn. There are some who will not come back as much as they should.

J: What are other reasons we come back at night?

M: One can come back to visit their loved ones. That is one of the reasons why people will have dreams of the person.

J: Is that the only time we come back, during our sleep time?

M: No. There are times when people can, and do, come back while awake. There are times that each of us will go through what is called a waking state of consciousness. That is one of the times where we become so relaxed that we allow our spirit part to travel to the other side.

J: We can receive glimpses of the other side at these times?

M: There are other times like the time when the body is in a complete state of total relaxation. There are many times when one will travel back to this side and later remember it.

J: So it must be important to go back to the other side?

M: Yes. It helps to keep that connection we all need.

J: Do you need that connection also?

M: Yes. We all do.

J: Why?

M: It makes us feel where we came from is important to our growth where we now are.

J: Is that why we have flask backs of our reincarnation?

M: Again, all things are not wasted.

J: All things are useful for our growth in this world?

M: And this world as well.

J: It looks like we are more complicated than most think.

M: People have not yet understood what they' re all about.

J: A lot us would like to learn more but are not sure where to go to get the Information.

M: All that information is within your reach. It is within.

J: When you say that all this information is within, are you talking about our souls?

M: Yes. Your soul is the storehouse of all knowledge and is used very little.

J: I know that we can communicate with our own soul. I had never thought of the idea of communicating with our souls until my Guide told me that I could, what she called, "activate the soul". In other words, talk to it, and by doing so, it will allow communication to start. This was all new to me and so one day I gave it a try to see what would happen. Sure enough, I found myself not only talking to my soul, but receiving a great deal of information from it.

M: Yes, and most people don’t even think of it.

J: There must be a lot of things that we here on the Earth plane don’t know about and things that we are capable of doing.

M: One of the problems is that most people don't know about it at all. They think they can only talk to their Spirit Guides.

J: Then we can learn a lot about ourselves by tuning into our souls. They know the future along with the past?

M: That is correct.

J: And therefore all knowledge is within all of us?

M: That is also correct, and the soul knows what one needs to know.

J: Should we talk to our soul only?

M: No, there is a time and a need to do so. The soul is the true you - the part that is connected to the source of all.

J: It appears that as humans we have the ability to know a great deal if we go within and make the connection with our souls.

M: That is right.

Soul communication is very important and must not be over looked in our effort to reach out to the world of spirit. Our soul is the one that truly knows us for who we are and where we are going while here on the Earth side of life. There are studies on spirit communication by many groups but not on the link with the soul. Perhaps in time, a study will begin with the role of the soul as a bridge between the level of the Earth and the world of spirit. Only time will tell.

"COMMUNICATION WITH LOVED ONES"

One question that keeps coming up with people who come in for a reading is "can I contact a loved one who is in spirit?" When I tell them that they are right beside them and still love them very much, that shocks them, and they look at me as if I were a little crazy.

The truth is that the world of spirit is so close to us that we can almost reach out and touch it. The only reason why we can't see or feel them is the fact that our worlds are separated by a rate of vibration. This acts as a barrier between them and us, but one that can be broken.

I would like to give an example so that you can get an idea of what I'm saying. If you were to take a fan and turn it on at a slow rate of speed you can easily see the blades, but as you increase the speed of the fan, it becomes harder and harder to see them. If the fan is spinning fast enough, the blades become almost completely invisible. That is the same way the spirit world appears to us here on the Earth side. Believe me, your loved ones are there, but the rate of vibration is much different than what we live with on the Earth Plane. We have to match their rate in order to make the connection.

In this chapter I ask Marion about the other side, and the ones who have passed to that world.

What follows is quite interesting.

J: Marion, there are a lot of people who go to a Medium in an attempt to make contact with their parent who has made the transition to your world. Can you explain why at times they may not be present at a reading?

M: Well, as you know, we have a life here, just as you do over on the side that you now occupy. Each one in time will have an assignment that they need to do. When a person comes in for a reading, the one that the person wanted to contact may be engaged in one of the assignments on their schedule.

J: So the fact that they, the ~~persons~~ loved ones, are not at the reading is in no way a statement that they do not love them?

M: Oh no, not at all, there is nothing but love here.

J: As you know, in the readings that I do, I try to be honest with my clients - so there will not be any misrepresentation in the reading.

M: Yes and that is the only way to be. If the parent is not there, do not make one up.

J: Yes, I understand.

M: The ones that you were looking for will come in, perhaps not in the reading that you are doing at the time. Perhaps some time later.

I read for a young woman who had lost her husband some time before, and wanted to make a connection with him. As it happened, the husband did show up at the time she came through the door of my office, staying with her throughout the entire time. This went on for several readings, but one day she came in for a scheduled reading without her husband beside her.

In the reading I was told that he would not be with her for a while, and that it was time for her to spread her wings and start a new life without him. I have to admit that I thought the husband would be with her that day, so it showed me not to expect anything, but to let spirit pull it through.

We are not alone in the scheme of things. Our loved ones, along with our personal Spirit Guides are there with us - and for us.

J: Marion, I have been told that if we want to communicate with our love ones, all we have to do is *simply* ask. Is that true?

M: The world of spirit is quite close to your world of material. We over here can and do hear you - as well as see the lights that emanate from you.

J: When this takes place do you and the others respond?

M: Yes, we are that close to each of you, and we attempt to reach you when we see or hear you. This is not easy, because most people will not respond to us being there with you.

J: I know there are some who doubt you are there, so they just ignore you.

M: We understand that. However, we keep on trying to of get you to hear.

J: It must be hard on your part - to keep doing this.

M: It is not easy; however we keep on trying to communicate with the hope to have you listen.

There are many methods of contacting your love ones from the spirit side of life, one being through the form called meditation, and the other is simply asking for your loved ones to be closer to you. My teacher, Gladys told me that all you have to do is call spirit three times and just listen to what they have to say. That seems easy, however, the lifestyle that we all have makes it difficult to take the time to even do that.

Our loved ones on the other side don't have a direct phone line. They don't need them. Just ask them - that is all it takes to get their attention. Your loved ones will come in to support you when you need them. They'll be there with a great deal of love. My partner, Trish, has been in my classes for some time and there were lots of times when I used to think she was failing asleep during, my class.

From time to time each one us gets what we call inspirations, or a feeling that we should pay attention to. They could be, in most cases, your Spirit Guide giving you some warning of impeding events.

"OH NO, NOT CASPER THE GHOST!"

In the Sunday papers there used to be a comic strip called "Casper the Friendly Ghost". Where this little loveable ghost would do all sorts of good deeds and still get into trouble. In real life there have been many stories of the haunting of homes, castles and even boats. There is some talk that the movie star John Wayne still walks the boat that he loved in life.

A while ago, I had a radio program called "The Spirit Connection", and I had guest speakers who were knowledgeable in Mediumship, Healing, and other related matters. This one evening, I wanted to talk on ghosts. In preparation for the show, I had the pleasure of visiting a well-known restaurant here in Florida where a spirit of a young girl is still looking for her father.

When I entered the stairway of this old restaurant I could feel the presence of something there with me. I later found out that where I felt this, was where the girl's spirit is usually felt.

Another time when something like this happened I was guarding a building. As I was doing, my watch, I had this heavy feeling of a presence of something there with me - like the one I had at the restaurant. I later found out there was a street person who was there for some time before passing over to spirit. There are too many of these ghost stories to simply rule out that there are no ghosts.

Marion had this to say about these Earth plane spirits, or ghosts.

J: Marion would you please tell me about ghosts? Do they exist or not?

M: Yes. These ghosts are staying in the places that they are used to.

J: So ghosts do exist?

M: Well, yes. But we do not call them ghosts. They are lost souls refusing to come back to the world they left.

J: Why would they not want to go back? Are they afraid to?

M: No, they are just-, as you would call it - misplaced in where they are.

J: I also heard that they do not want to leave the Earth plane because they were materialistic. Is that true?

M: Yes. There are some who will refuse to come back to the world of spirit because of the materialistic things they acquired there on the Earth side.

J: Do they mean any harm to those who are in their homes or other places?

M: As a general rule, no, however, there are still some who will do everything to protect their property. Those who have that mind set are the ones who will take a long time to learn once here.

J: Will they eventually go back?

M: Yes. Time heals all things, and at the right time, they will come back.

J: So it appears we, whether over on you're side, or here on the Earth, have choices to make?

M: Yes. Each has choices to make - in either place.

J: I know of a situation where a friend had a ghost who was bothering her. I told her what to do, and the spirit went back to the light of the world of spirit.

M: Yes. That will happen from to time, depending on the state of mind of both.

J: So, can we lower ourselves to a level that will bring these on?

M: Doesn't that happen to you? When things are not going to well, you drop your guard and you allow these matters enter you area?

J: That is true. So what you are saying is that we can bring these ghosts who are not good for us into our area if we do not watch it?

M: Well sure. If you pray or ask for protection all the time, the best will come your way.

J: I had a woman mention to me the other day that she knows there is a ghost in the home she is about to visit and she wanted to get to know the spirit. I told her that she must first protect herself before she does that.

M: Yes, it is better to be safe than sorry.

A few years ago I was teaching a new class to a new group of students where I was residing in Massachusetts. One of the students became disturbed by the fact he had the spirit of a friend who passed some years ago. The spirit kept coming into the room and disrupting the class to the point that everyone was ready to jump ship and leave. I managed to quiet the group down and desired to see for myself what they were talking about. We decided to hold hands, stay in a circle, find the lost soul, and help him to find his way home towards the light.

I must admit that I thought at first one of the students was playing a trick on me, until we made contact with the spirit. It was just as one of the members had described the spirit right down to the loss of an arm during the accident. I asked the class to follow my instructions in the attempt to help this spirit and in a matter of time we managed to help the spirit to find the light and out of the class into the spirit side. It was interesting not only for me, but for the class as well. The experience gave us all a good understanding of how we can, and that night did, help a lost soul to find its way home.

There are many instances of sightings that occur in different places all over the world. On many occasions, I have had the opportunity of either sensing a spirit, or helping others in dealing with them.

When I came to Florida I became a security guard and was assigned to an old building that was under construction. I was alone one night and was in the process of doing my rounds, when I had a feeling that someone was with me in the building. I knew there was no one there except me. This was this same feeling that I had at the restaurant. As I was walking through that empty building, one of my classmates from high school, (who was killed in Vietnam in the late seventies) appeared and stood beside me in the same way that he used to when he was with me in school.

To be quite honest with you, Mike took me by surprise, and I asked him why he was there that night. I remember him saying he came to protect me, even if I felt that I was protecting him.

As time went on, I could hear the voice of the entrapped spirit. There was a ghost in the building. It was later verified when another security guard, who left because of it, never went back into that building.

"HARPS OF THE ANGELS"

Angels with large wings and playing harps while watching over each of us as we travel the path of life, is a picture that most of us have of these angelic beings from heaven. In many books they' re referred to as messengers, who will come to the help those in need.

I remember Jimmy Stewart, one of the great movie actors of his day, where he played this desperate man in need of help, ready to end his life by jumping off a bridge into the murky water of the river. As he stepped to the edge of the bridge, this old gentleman came to his side and saved him in the nick of time. This stranger was an angel trying to earn his wings, by performing one last attempt to save someone's life after his failing on several attempts to help his fellow man.

Although this was a movie, and ended in a happy note (as most movies do), could this be the way the angels appear to us in our time of our desperation?

There are many people who will stake all that they have on it. In most religions, angels are a part of the understanding of the connection to our God. In a strange way, they truly are God's messengers of his words and acts of compassion to the world. Is this a real happening or is it a myth that has been devised by man in the attempt to reach out for something that he cannot explain? With the help of Marion, we will explore the life of the angels and their purpose here on the Earth side, as well as their existence in the world of spirit.

J: I know that we have angels with us, but what are they like?

M: First of all they do exist, and are around each of you who reside on the Earth side of life.

J: One of the questions is, "do they have wings at all?"

M: No. There is no need to have wings here in the spirit side, for we all have to do is to travel by thought.

J: I thought so.

M: And you are right in your thinking.

J: So if the angels do not have wings, then why are they depicted that way?

M: That goes back to the ancient times, and how people wanted to see them.

J: What is the purpose of the angels?

M: To work with the ones they are assigned to.

J: Are they special in the way? Are they closer to the source, or God?

M: We are all special to the source and no one is excluded.

J: Are the angels in a special place in the spirit side of life?

M: No more then we are. Again no one is any more special than the next. Here, we are all quite special - as you and the others are in your world. You understand, John, we are all workers in the sources understanding of what we have to do to support each other as we travel our paths of existence.

J: I know that they do intervene in our affairs.

M: Every day they enter in to each person's life.

J: How do they do that?

M: Not as winged entities. At times they may look like the humans on the Earth – so you will never know who they are.

J: There have been many cases where people need help and someone would come in from nowhere, help the person, and then just leave - never to be seen again. Would this be an angel?

M: A lot of times, yes. There are times when a spirit will take on the human form to come in and help the person who needs their help.

J: After all these years, I did not know that spirit could do that.

M: Yes, and why not?

J: I don't know.

M: There are a lot of things that you don't know.

J: I guess you're right.

M: There are times when your angels come to you and you don't know it.

J: How should we contact them?
M: Just ask and you will receive.
J: Will there be times when we will see them?
M: As a Medium, you should see them most of the time in your readings.
J: What about the other times?
M: There are times when people will see them.
J: Then people who do will say that they have wings. Why is that?
M: We want people to understand the difference between spirits and angels, and the best way is to have people see them in the way that they are accustomed.
J: And that would be with wings?
M: Correct. The most important thing to know, is the fact that they are there each of you.
J: Yes.
M: The angel world is a big help to human kind.
J: I know that. My other half had an angel help her.
M: Yes, that is what they do. I was also there that day.
J: Do angels have names?
M: Don't you?
M: We have names, just as you do on the Earth. In fact angels take their names from where they come from.
J: Where do angles come from?

M: Both from the Earth side and from other worlds.

J: The other worlds would make another book, but there are angels from here on the Earth side?

M: Yes, and they have been here for many years and moved to different levels while over here.

J: So the angels are a highly develop soul?

M: To some degree.

J: Will you become an angel?

M: I have a long way to go, but in the right time, yes.

J: So one must have to go through a lot of growth in order to elevate to that level.

M: It would seem to be a lot of growth but that is not true either.

J: What does it take to be an angel?

M: A great deal of love - more than one would know.

J: You have a lot of love. I believe that.

M: Thank you. However I have a long way to go.

J: I know that you will make it.

M: We will see.

J: Love is a thing that we must learn.

M: That is quite true - and that love with your neighbors in the world is what it takes to keep peace.

M: I know what you are about to ask, and yes, part of the job of the angel is to help bring in this peace for the Earth before it is too late.

J: I guess that they have their work cut out for them.

M: Yes, that is for sure.

J: Can we ask for our own personal angel's help?

M: Yes. Just ask, and they will be there with you.

J: How will we know when they are with us?

M: Some people will see them or they will sense their presence.

J: I guess whatever way; we must have faith in the fact that they are here to support us in our lives.

M: Yes, big time if we listen to them.

Many years ago, when I was a child, I had my first encounter with an angel who stayed with me. Over these years, from time to time, I still think of the encounter. I remember to this day where I was at the time. That is how clear the happening was. It was a clear day and I was playing with some of my friends when I looked into the sky and saw this beautiful angelic being over my head. I'm not sure how old I was at the time; however I remember how it struck me. I never saw that angel or any thing that resembled one since, at least not in that form. I now see them more in the spiritual form, through my Mediumship. One thing that I know is true is the fact that they do exist and are there for each of us as we move through life.

As Marion said, we have encounters each day with our angels and don't even know it, or even think about them until we run into some problems that warrant their help. Stop and think about it for a moment, what you may have encountered that were just a little out of the norm. Perhaps there was something that just came up out of nowhere and hit you on the head with some new idea or something that you never even thought of. Like a rush out of the night, it comes to you and it works!

Perhaps it was something that you were working on and ran in to a block. Then one day a so-called brainstorm came in and you said, "Why, I didn't even think of that approach before!" Where do you think the great inventors receive their ideas? Is it just luck or a touch of brilliance? Perhaps it's their angel tapping on their shoulder with some new idea.

So the next time some brainstorm hits you, don't just shrug it off. It could be one of you're angels telling you to pay attention to what they are telling you.

"SOUL LIGHTS "

When I get a chance, I take a moment for myself and just tune into the world of spirit and my guides who are always with me. I receive a great deal of interesting information from them, some of the information I don't want to know and then there is some that I need.

One of the times that I was in this state, I was told about the function of our soul and just how important it is for each of us to be able to tune into it and use it each day of our lives. My guide was quite insistent about the fact that the soul can do so much for us if only we would just listen and talk to it. To me that sounded a little strange; however, I try to do what my guides tell me to do.

I had no idea the soul once activated can relay information back, giving the necessary steps to take throughout life along with our past experience.

I know what you are thinking, "What talking soul? Give me a break". Those were my words when my guides told me that. However, the soul does communicate with you when you take the time to ask it to do so.

I had placed this information on the back burner until taking the time to sit down and do this book. Perhaps this is the right time to bring these facts to the forefront so all can learn that we have many means to work with while here on Earth.

It is interesting that today I was struggling with a topic to use and was about to give up for a while with the hope that later I would be able to start up again. I was getting a glimpse of Marion around me saying to start writing, so here I am with pen in hand ready to go. The following is what she had to say about our soul and it's function.

J: Okay and I guess the new topic is on the soul?

M: This would be a good time to bring it up, so others will understand.

J: I know that each of us has a soul but what is its function?

M: I think the best question would be "What's not its function"

J: So it must have many?

M: The soul of each has a great deal to do with you, for it is the real you.

J: Is that what you see from where you are the lights of the soul?

M: Correct. Each light from the soul tells us how you are and where you are located, along with the problems that you are going through at the time.

J: Would these lights emanating from us be like the so-called Aura?

M: Yes.

J: And those in the world of spirit can read these lights?

M: Yes. Each of us can tell a great deal about a person from their lights that are coming our way.

J: So these lights shine towards you?

M: Yes. The lights will point towards us here in the spirit side.

J: You must see us as a ray of lights and not as a person form where you are.

M: It depends on where we are at the time. If you are close, we can make you out. If we are not that close, we see the lights shining brightly from where you are.

J: Does everything emit light here on the Earth side?

M: Everything. So that you know, that includes trees, plants, and even rocks.

J: So you know where every thing is on the Earth?

M: Yes. Everything.

J: If a person has an illness can you detect that?

M: Yes, and we send someone to be there with them.

J: You mention that the aura and the soul lights are close as far as what they look like, is that fair to say?

M: Very close, but there is a difference between the two - and we can see the difference.

J: That must be quite the thing to tell the differences between the two. Can we here on Earth learn the difference?
M: Sure, if you have the right one to teach you. This is one of the reasons we only give your world just so much information.
J: Is that because of the ego that is still here?
M: The ego can be quite damaging to one who thinks he knows all the answers.
J: How long did it take you to learn all this information?
M: Not that long. It is up to the one who wants to learn and their rate of consciousness.
J: Can we get a jump-start from here on the Earth?
M: Yes. It is up to the person who is willing to learn.

"THE SPIRIT COUNCIL"

Marion mentioned to me about the council that resides on the other side. A number of older souls are there to help us to make preparation for the Earth journey and back. This group of loving entities is instrumental in helping the ones who want to make the trip back to the Earth side with the right plan and a guide who is committed to the person making the journey. A blueprint, or map, is drawn up and accepted by the council. It includes the choice of parents, along with many other choices, so the new soul will become adjusted a little easier.

There are a lot of preparations that are made before one is allowed to come back. Since I started this writing, one of the council members has made a point to come to me on several occasions to talk to me about the matters that I need do in order to grow spiritually in my work.

The following discussion is what my guide Marion had to say on the subject of the council.

J: First of all, is there a council in the world of spirit?

M: Yes,

J: What is their function?

M: There are many things that the council will do.

J: Is it true that they help in the planning of the new arrivals to the Earth side?

M: Yes, as well as the journey back to this side. They also help in the selection of the parents that the soul makes its entry to.

J: So our parents are selected before birth? I have heard of this from some of my guides, and know it must be right that there is a council who is able to work with the new spirits that want to come back to the Earth plane, perhaps also to other distant worlds as well. It could also be that this council helps us to reach other levels that we need to reach while here on the Earth.

M: Correct. The soul, depending on what it needs, will elect to go to the parents who either will help the soul to grow, or to support the parents they elected to be with.

J: We must have some type of master plan for each of us drawn before we come here to the Earth side.

M: Each soul has a map or a plan that is submitted to the council for approval before it is allowed to come to the Earth side.

J: So our whole life is planned out?

M: One can, and does, make changes in their course of events along the path of life.

J: Are these changes free will?

M: No. They are just the choices that one can make.

J: If we make these choices, and go in the wrong direction - will the council help us to get back on track?

M: Yes. There will be an attempt to help the soul to move in the right direction if, and only if - the soul of the person will listen.

J: That seems to be a problem with most of us.

M: Big time.

J: What else does the council do?

M: That's enough don't you think?

J: Well, Yes. However I believe there is more.

M: They do appear on your Earth side at times when needed.

J: They come to help us?

M: Yes, all the time. That is why they are busy.

J: I saw one of the council members a while ago, and he has been with me from time to time. Will this happen to others?

M: That depends on what's in store for the one who they are visiting. Not all people will have council member visit.

J: Can you explain?

M: It depends on the level of the person, and if they're helping their fellow person.

J: What about the ones who are at a lower level?

M: The ones who are on the lower levels will still receive help but not from council for theirs is a different need.

J: So one is on a spiritual level and the other is on a material level. Is that right?
M: Correct.

"WHAT IS YOUR LEVEL?"

What I have learned is that I am still learning, and at times it is hard to do. We should learn something new each day of our lives. In some of my communications with Spirit about the other side and things of interest to me, I have learned there are a many different levels that we as mediums, are working on. Perhaps it is only one or two steps higher than this one. In order to break through to the different levels that separate us from the other side, it is the rates of vibration that come into play. This is where, as far as we know to date, everything in the universe vibrates, despite the fact that we cannot usually see these vibrations. These vibrations are invisible to the naked eye.
Levels are, from what I have been told, different steps we go through when we are ready. By the way, there are too many to even think of - let alone measure in numbers. I must admit that after all these years of Mediumship, I never knew about levels until I sat down at the computer and started to write this book. With a lack of information on the topic of levels, I once again turned to my Spirit Guide for some of the interpretations of levels and how they apply to us here on Earth and on the other side. I once again walked the beach as I attempt to do each day, and asked for help with the book. It was on such a day that Gladys, one of my closest guides and a helper, came in. I guess it was to give me

the lecture that I needed that day. She talked to me about the different types of levels that are a part of existence as well as what these levels have to do with each of us and our growth, both here and on the other side.

Knowing the way Gladys was while on-the Earth, quick with her words, I had a hard time keeping, up with her. She came forth with the knowledge of these levels. She mentioned to me that we on the Earth would have a hard time with understanding these levels because we look at things in a way of Earth measurements and that is not really applicable.

For example: a half level is not what it sounds like. If placed on a tape measure it would be shown as a half inch, where in fact, it is some distant more. Perhaps it is along, the idea of many miles in Earth measurements. In a way, I can understand what she is saying about these levels. In this part of the text I ask Gladys more about these levels and their role both here and in the world of spirit. I started out in this chapter with the intent of having Marion help me in this, but Gladys stepped in to add her support and that is fine with me. Both of them have a good understanding of the matter at hand. Gladys was one of my teachers while she was still on the Earth plane, and she helped me in my understanding of Mediumship. Now that she has passed into the other side, she has continued to be with me in my work.

J: Gladys, would you please tell us about levels?

G: First of all, levels are like steps in the sky.

J: These are invisible steps?

G: To some, yes.

J: You mean that we can see them?

G: And why not?

J: I never thought that we here on the Earth could see this.

G: People who are spiritually evolved can see a great deal.

J: That's true, however for the ones who cannot at this time see these levels, would you explain them to us?

G: As I said, they are like stairs that go in all different directions - and not always just up.

J: These levels are like a crisscross through the universe?

G: And beyond.

J: I read once that the spirit world is about three feet above the world that we now live in. Is that right?

G: That is a level that some live on. There are others that live on much higher levels.

J: Okay, on the beach today you mentioned that a half level is not what we think is half, but could be a distance of a mile. Is that correct?

G: Yes, remember that our measurements are greatly different than yours on the Earth side.

J: Would it be right to say that a light year would be a full level?

G: Your measurement of a light year is again different than the one over here. A light year is not one level, but many.

J: When we move to these different levels, do we receive more information about Spirit life?

G: Yes.

J: By traveling to these different levels, do we obtain different Spirit Helpers?

G: Why, sure. Each level that one travels to, the more refined they become.

J: Can we reach these levels here on the Earth?

G: Yes, all the time.

J: There must be ways to obtain these levels here. How do we do that?

G: By tuning into the world of spirit and listening to what is being said. That will be the hardest thing of all to do. LISTENING!

"WHICH IS WHICH?"

Some people have used the words "Spirit Guides" and "Spirit Helpers" interchangeably over the years; however, there are grave differences between the two.

Each of us has both, and at times, more than several will be around adding, their support to us as we confront some difficult issues we need to deal with. The workings of these wonderful support groups are a story in itself, and I don't have the time or the pages to offer it to you here.

One of the questions that I was asked recently is my father my Spirit Guide? I will ask Marion that important question for it is one that is on the minds of many of the people who go for readings. Rather than hearing the answer to this question from me, I'll let Marion tell you.

J: I believe that in order to clear this up, we must discuss these two.

M: Well yes, but it is okay to use the words in the way that one wants.

J: True, however, there are some who would like to know the true difference.

M: I will go over the two for you and your readers.

J: Thank you.

M: First, let me start with what you call "Spirit Guides". A Spirit Guide is one who is assigned to you in the world of spirit and before you come to the Earth side. Both are reviewed with things to expect.

J: Is there more than one who comes with you?

M: As you have found out today, there is more than one.

J: On the first day of August 2002, I found myself with another Spirit Guide, one with the name of Little Bear, a young child a Native American Indian boy. I had no idea that he would be with me, and that this little Indian boy would be one of my guides. I was under the impression that each of us had only one guide. We do come to the Earth plane with two or more guides, each with different functions for us. Is that right?

M: Yes. Guides have his or her work cut out for them, with the one that they came with.

J: Marion, what are the functions of the guide?

M: A guide is one who is quite close to you, and remains there for you until you both come back to the world of spirit- as I mentioned earlier. The guide does try to intervene in the decisions that you make.

J: Does this mean that once the plan is set up in the spirit side; the guide more or less helps you to stay on that track?

M: Yes. And as one moves off the path, the guide will pull them in line, or will try to do so anyway.

J: There are some people who will not listen?

M: Yes John, as you well know.

J: Quite

There have been times that even I have doubted the existence of these helpers and would at times just believe that the information was coming from me and not from anyone else. How wrong I have been on that.

M: The guide will do all that it can to speak to the one who they are with, and attempt to get their attention. Sometimes it could be just a written word that will make the person say, "Well perhaps that isn't me."

J: Is it like a book falling off of a shelf and it is the book that the person must read?

M: That happens many times.

J: I know it has happened to me a lot. When I go to the bookstore, somehow a book will keep getting my attention.

M: These spirits works in funny ways to get your attention.

J: I know, and that is the hard part to understand - that the same neat people are supporting us over there in the world of spirit.

M: We come with love and we want to help each of you.

J: Yes I believe that.

M: Once people can understand that this is the true reason we enter the Earth plane. It is through love and to help them as one travels their path on the Earth.

J: The Spirit Guide is one who, lets say, watches over us like a guardian angel. Would that be correct?

M: To some point, yes.

J: I am sure there is more.

M: Yes. The guide is also the one who will not only attempt to keep you on the right path, but to have you to stay with the plan you both worked on before you came to the Earth side.

J: Let's go back to that part where the guide and the individual were in the Spirit World. What takes peace as far as developing the so-called plan?

M: That is a good question. The guide and the one who wants to come back to the Earth side go before the council for a review of the reasons for coming back and how this will help the soul, or you save the individual.

J: Then what happens?

M: Both the soul and the guide obtain permission from the council, and then they can travel back.

J: Again the soul and guide must have a plan?

M: Yes.

J: Does the plan have in it what is to be accomplished while on the Earth?
M: To some degree, yes.
J: The guide and the soul must know one anothe
M: Sometimes the guide will decide to come with a new soul and take up residence with that soul.
J: So the assignment is not that easy to make?
M: We don't always get the assignment to the one they would like to.

If the Spirit Guide has all that and perhaps more then what do the Spirit Helpers do in our lives while here on the Earth? Here again, I turn to Marion in order to ascertain the correct answer to the question. The following is what is revealed in my conversation with her.

J: Marion, the information that you gave me on the purpose of the Spirit Guide is very interesting. Now may I ask you about Spirit Helpers?
M: Yes, go for it.
J: What is the function of the Spirit Helpers?
M: The Spirit Helper is very important to the one who they go to.
J: In what way?
M: In many ways the helper, unlike the Spirit Guide who you just talked about, is

one who will come in to support you in the time that you need them.

J: Is it true that unlike the Spirit Guide, the Spirit Helper is one who is not assigned to you at birth?

M: That is quite true. The Spirit Helper is one that becomes close to you while on the Earth plane.

J: The Spirit Guide is one who we may not know on the other side?

M: You very well may not, but in some cases you will know the one who will come to support you. Here again, the guide is the one who is assigned to you before you arrive on the Earth - staying with you until you head back home to the other side.

"YOUR CHART OF LIFE"

Like a ship in the night, the chart on the Captains table is the only way home to a safe haven and the port of call. I enjoy the sea and when I was younger, I wanted to go to sea. I longed for the adventure it offered to the seamen who followed its currents and the new distant islands that were there over the horizon. If you had a boat, and started out in an attempt to reach a distant shore, you would have to study the many facets of the ocean - it's tides and the wind along with the currents.

On our journey to the Earth, did we have to do the same thing? Did we study the way from there to this place we now call our temporary home? This is one of the perplexing questions that need to be answered. And if so, what other information did we obtain before we arrived here on the Earth plane? Or was it just the luck of the draw? How do our families and friends come into play in our Earth life? How is this done, and by whom? The answer may seem too obvious to be a question, however, as we will soon see there are many other elements that play into the answers.

These are some of the questions that we will take up in this chapter with the help of Marion who will (I hope) answer these and other questions that are of interest. I want to state that I am not a fatalist. I don't believe that someone orchestrates our whole lives, as if we are puppets on a string. However, I do believe that there has to be some form of a plan, or script that we follow for the purpose of growth while here on the material side of life.

I set up questions to ask Marion, knowing that I would receive the correct answers on the subject at hand. It was early in the morning when I sat down to start this chapter with the confidence that one of my guides would be with me to start the work. I believed that just perhaps they would not be awake this early in the day. To my surprise and delight, Marion was ready to start. The next for me was to stay awake and ready for the information to come through.

J: Marion, The other day you mentioned to me about our life s chart, or a book of what is to be expected of us while on our visit on the Earth plane. Is that right?

M: That is correct.

J: What does this chart or book have in it?

M: The things one must do while on the Earth.

J: Everything?

M: Yes.

J: Can you give us some example of what you mean?

M: Sure. A person may elect to go to the Earth plane as a worker, or a teacher. That is decided upon before going.

J: Are there any reasons for that choice?

M: Yes. There is always a reason, as I have said before nothing is ever-wasted - either in our world or yours. Let me tell you that by choosing the person you want to be, you are learning while on the Earth plane.

J: Can we make changes along the way?

M: If it is in the chart.

J: So there are times that we can make changes?

M: One can make changes at any time if you want to.

I later found out that in our life, there are different times when we can get out (or off) the Earth plane. These are at our own option and some take the option and leave.

J: That is interesting. Can you tell me at what times in our lives these occur?

M: That depends on the person's book or chart.

J: Does the council on your side set up these rules that govern different events in our lives here on the Earth?

M: Source governs all, however, the council will establish what is designed by the Source you call God and make sure that the ones going back to the Earth follow the design.

J: If we start out in life and then later make a change to create a new direction in our life, is that also part of the chart of our life?
M: Yes, in most cases. That is in the book or an effect of the chart that refers to our life. Each one who goes back to the Earth has within him/her the ability to make some corrections in their life. All this information is in the chart, or what we over here call the book of events that pertains to each life.
J: In time we get back on the right track?
M: Sometimes. There are some people who will never get back on track.
J: Why?
M: There are some that will neither listen nor heed what has been written.
J: Does this book of effects tell what will happen to the individual each day?
M: The book is so accurate that it can give you the seconds in the life of an
Individual.
J: You know as I am writing this second, I had no idea this book of effects was that accurate. I thought it would apply to just the total life of the person?
M: See? Even you can learn something new.
J: I guess. This book of effects takes us on a second by second march through life. Do we have any way of understanding it?
M: The soul of each does. That is why the soul is there – (Remember the chapter on the soul) along with other reasons to support

us in life and it sharpens grips of the Earth itself.

In the text, there is a connection between the soul and the book of effects, or what I have called the chart of our lives. Perhaps the soul is the storehouse of the information that is our blueprint for the way we travel while here on the Earth plane. There is a strong urge to ask how one contacts the soul in the attempt to obtain this information. With that in mind, I asked Marion how we could reach our own souls in the effort to help us understand more about ourselves.

J: Marion I know that you and I have at times discussed the issue of the soul, and how one can communicate with it.

M: Yes.

J: If the soul holds all the information about ourselves, how do we obtain this information?

M: The soul does have all that is needed to help you on your path - if you would learn to pay attention to what it is saying to you.

J: Is there any special way that we can communicate with our souls?

M: No.

J: Then what is the best way?

M: Just ask, as I mentioned before.

J: You mean ask the soul to start talking to you?

M: That is all that you do, is just talk.

J: To some of us that sounds quite strange to do.
M: Why? That is just you, and the ones that think that way. The way of the Source is quite easy. You on the Earth plane make it hard.
J: The more that I get in involved in this, the more I understand.
M: Just don't change your mind on that.

"WHY THE SOUL CHOSE EARTH"

What is the attraction to this planet that we, as souls, travel here in the first place? Our Solar System consists of nine planets stretching from Mercury, and out to the East one, Pluto. That one is a small planet, and is the last planet found to date. There are some scientists who believe the Solar System has another object or planet out beyond Pluto. They' re basing this on what seems to be an effect on Pluto. Perhaps this could be the tenth planet? Time and more studies will give us the answer to that question.

Out of these nine, we choose the third planet from the sun, called Earth, and come here as souls incarnate. We reside here to better our lives or learn something to improve it.

It is true, of all the planets that we are aware of, the Earth is the only one that is conducive to the human race in the form we are now using. We are souls in nature, and as souls, we can go anywhere within the Solar System - even beyond and into even more distant places, if we wanted.

Is it possible that the Earth is a place to learn, as most believe, or are we here for another reason? There must be some explanation to the scheme of things. If so, what is it? With all these questions to be answered, I turned again to Marion for her help and assistance.

J: I'd like to ask you why "the Earth - why here?"

M: That one is simple to answer. Each planet in your system has a different function and the Earth has the one of learning.

J: Is it true what I have read. We come back to learn from our mistakes.

M: Not really.

J: Then why do we come back to the Earth plane?

M: One comes back to the Earth plane, if they elect to do so, in an attempt to add on their knowledge they already know.

J: When we add on to what we know, are you saying each time we come back to the Earth we are growing?

M: Of course we are growing. In each encounter with the Earth, we are learning. One keeps learning, as we do over here in the world of spirit.

J: What do we learn?

M: The purpose is to enhance oneself to become better.

J: To become better how?

M: Spiritually. People on the Earth must learn that they have to become more spiritual in nature and not so much in material matters.

J: I understand, however we here must earn enough to live.

M: That is quite true. Don't forget, I was there for some time before I came here, so I do understand the need to work and earn enough to live. The spiritual path still must be the one to follow in all that you do.

J: It is hard to balance both.

M: No. That is not true. One can, and must, balance the two

J: You sound very solid on this matter.

M: Yes, and there is a good reason for that statement.

J: And what is that?

M: Your world, as you know it, is changing and the part that is making it change is the ego that it is not seeing. People need to get back to the spiritual path.

J: That may be true, however some of us are into living with ego in a big way and perhaps cannot get out from under.

M: That is just an excuse. People can get out of their situation if they want to.

J: I believe you are right.

M: Yes, I know that I am on that matter. It's up to each one of you to make the necessary changes.

One thing about Marion is she was a very smart woman and knows her stuff when it comes to Spiritual matters. Marion was very close to my guide Gladys and I am sure they talked about many of these topics while on the Earth - and now in the spirit world. In the course of my Mediumship I have been lucky to talk to both on subjects that pertain to each of us here on the Earth.

"REINCARNATION: THE END: OR IS IT?"

I had a call one day from a woman who was confused about her religion. She loved her faith and the church she was attending. One thing bothered her, though. Her religion did not believe in reincarnation.

Today there are many people from different religious backgrounds who believe in the concept of reincarnation and that we have come here to the Earth plane more than once.

In one of my many talks with my guides, I was told that I was a monk in the fourteenth and fifteenth Century in England. They told me I left the order and later went back to it - for reasons I will not at this time get into.

This statement was not shocking to me, for in my last year of high school, I was intending to enroll in the seminary and follow the life of a priest. I can just see it now - Father John.

There are many cases where people will have a feeling that they have been in a different country, or have done something that had no experience with in this life. Could these be past life memories that come flowing into their present lives?

I feel we do come back to the Earth on many occasions for one reason or another. Perhaps we return to obtain additional knowledge we need to know. Maybe it's to have a reunion with someone that who wasn't ready in the previous lifetime. In my case it was the interest in the history of monks. It's something I have been interested in for years. That agrees with the experiences of many others who have had similar feelings of past life experience:

I don't believe that we were all king and queens of some exotic country, but each of us has had our share of being a common man in a past life.

At the time that I started this writing it was 5:42 in the morning and Marion was here with me.

J: Marion is it true about reincarnation?
M: As to what?
J: That it does exist?
M: Yes, of course.
J: So most of us have had many lives here on the Earth?
M: Yes, and elsewhere.
J: Marion, is it true reincarnation has a lot to do with us as a total person?
M: Yes. In a way, each person is the total of all past, present, and future experience.
J: You mean our soul has all these wrapped up inside each of us?

M: Correct. Each soul has all the knowledge.

J: Marion, can we recall our past lives while in the physical body?

M: Yes, if you reach your soul

J: You mean talk to our own souls?

M: Yes, as we have mentioned before

J: I still say that is hard to do?

M: No it is quite easy once you learn how.

J: Once we contact our souls, how will the past help us in the present?

M: When you know what you are all about, then you will understand yourself better.

J: Marion do we come back to learn, or to pick up where we left off?

M: A little of both.

J: When we come back to the Earth side, we acquire more knowledge to bring with us for the next return.

M: Each soul always learns.

J: Yes, that would make sense.

M: There is a knowledge each of us will always retain and carry over each time we come here.

J: Is it important to come back to the Earth?

M: Not always, only if you expect to come back.

J: We have a choice to come back?

M: Yes, each has a choice to come back to the Earth or anywhere you want to travel. Each one of us is given choices - even on the Earth.

It would appear that reincarnation is a fact, and not a myth, as some would have us believe. The soul does come back to the Earth side many.

Many years ago, the original Late Show host was Johnny Carson. Most of us remember him for his wit and the different celebrities that came on his snow. Some became today's super stars.

During his commercial breaks he would say, "We'll be right back." without knowing it, perhaps this statement was quiet intuitive. Perhaps coming back is one of the keys to ourselves, and the knowledge that we will do it all over again.

"ANGELS"

One thing I always wanted to see was an Angel. I think at times a lot of other children wanted the same view. One bright day, I was playing with friends, when I remember looking up at the sky and seeing what I thought was a beautiful Angel. It was at such a height that it was hard to make her out, but I had the feeling it was an angel.

I recall after that day I wanted to become a priest and follow the religion. Perhaps it was the Angels effect on me. It was the first and only time these eyes have looked upon an Angel. When I got older, I started to reflect on my youth, and looked forward to sighting the Angel again as I searched for some spiritual meaning. I suspect it comes from the desire to be closer to our creator, and to know we are important to him.

The interest in Angels has been with us for thousands of years, and Angels have been depicted in all forms of art that adorn literature and the walls of churches all over the world.

In my youth, my church also had Angels on the stained glass windows, which glowed with the light of the sun shining through them. If you looked closely, you could feel that the Angels moved. With the advent of television shows such as "Touched by an Angel" and the number of books on the subject filling bookstore shelves, the interest in Angels grows, and it tells us Angels are still on the minds of each of us.

People are becoming more exposed to the concept of the Angel world and many are accepting the fact we are not alone. Some of the questions that most people ask are, "Do Angels really exist", and 'Where are they when you need one" and "How do they come into the scheme of things as far as our world goes?" There are people who will tell you they have their Angel with them all the time, as they travel through life. They picture them with beautiful large glowing wings that extend some distance out from their bodies. Its interesting - most people will not mention that their Angel has a harp!

People describe many Angels with different names, but one of the main Angels is Michael, who seems to be with everyone at the same time. It is a good thing Michael is a multi-dimensional Angel, or he would have a difficult time being all these places at the same time. It is not to say there is not a Michael who is an Angel, and that he is with someone doing his work. In my readings, when people ask me if their Angel is with them, if I can see one, I will mention it - if not, I will not.

I haven't seen an Angel around anyone while doing readings for along time. This was not to say the person didn't have one. I believe I just didn't pay too much attention to the fact they were around. It wasn't until I came to Florida and I started seeing Angels around people frequently. Perhaps it hadn't been the right time before for me to see them. Spirit will give only what you are ready for, and it's the only explanation that I can offer. Another factor is religion. With a religious upbringing, we expect to see Angels. I try to avoid that path, and not allow my mind to play into it.

Until my experiences in Florida, I had to be convinced of their existence - as I have always done over the last twenty years of this work. After my first encounter I began to understand a new world, one that, up until then, was a little foreign to me.

I have since changed my mind about these wonderful helpers and the magnificent beauty, which emanates from them, as well as the splendor of their support. They now show themselves quite often in my readings. In the readings, they come in as being of different ages and sexes, from the young to the old, including children. As my guide and I have become more refined in working with them, they appear more often.

The knowledge I have learned lately is the fact the Earth is in need of help, and many of these angelic helpers are coming in to assist us in this effort. Another thing I have been told by my guides is that some of the angels are now walking among us, assisting us without our knowledge. This was difficult for me to accept at first, until, when talking to some people about their experiences, I found myself hearing it has happened to them. Their stories strengthen the realization there are more angelic forces present now than ever before.

There are stories in which people have been in disastrous occurrences in their lives. In their greatest time of need, a stranger came out of nowhere to assist them, and left as suddenly as he or she came. Despite these events, the question always comes up most often, "Are there Angels walking here on the Earth?" My own feeling is there are indeed angelic forces among us today and they will continue to be here for many years to come. I can say this because my Spirit Guides have helped me understand angels and the purposes that bring them here. Each of us has travel to the Earth plane with our own Guardian Angel who will be with us as we make the return trip home to the spirit world and our loved ones who went before us.

Some people say they have with them archangels with well-known names, or with a high vibration, which will carry them through the world without any problems, and therefore they don't have to worry about anything. I can't be sure about that statement. I have read for many people, an Angel may appear, but it will not be one of the "magnificent " Angels or of the high force which people tend to expect.

This is not to say others will not have such an angel around them, as its very possible. We draw what is needed at the time.

Since I have moved to Florida, the encounters with angels have grown to the point that I encounter them most of the time during a reading. I am open to all possibilities when it comes to this work.

There is another question I myself have wondered about and am often asked,: "Do Angels have those beautiful wings that are depicted in literature and art?"

I know in the world of spirit, the mode of travel is thought. All a spirit has to do to get from one place to another is simply think where it wants to be there, and it happens. Wouldn't it be neat if we could do that? If it were true that entities travel in this manner, then it would be safe to assume angels also travel the same way.

In my readings, I see the "wings" that encompass the Angels as they hover around the one I am reading for, but there appears to be more of an "AURA" effect emerging from the Angels than the wings we are used to thinking about. I have asked my guides about wings of the angels, and they told me that it is the soul energy or the Auric energy that one sees.

Angels are from a higher vibration level and they don't need wings to travel from one place to another, and that correlates to what my guides tell me. From what we know about the world of spirit and space itself, there is no air. This would mean there is no means of propulsion, as we know it, and no physical body, allowing them to go where no one has ever gone before. Angels more closely resembled spirit. As such, they have no physical body. Their "body" is more like a mist, or as one of my spirit guides explained, "like shredded paper". That is how thin their bodies appear. It is the form that gives them the flexibility of flight.

As I have mentioned before, I feel that there are Angels on the Earth side even now, and that they are here to help us. A few years ago there was a picture out titled, "Oh God", starring George Burns and John Denver. George portrayed God and had a hard time convincing people he was God, because like all of us, they wanted all kinds of proof, such as the Earth shaking or snow falling in the middle of the summer. If you can picture George dressed in his old cap and smoking a large cigar, it would be very difficult to believe he was God. Who knows, he might be the way God would make the next appearance to us on the Earth! Some of us have the notion the next time God comes to the Earth, he will appear as fire and riding a white horse.

So, we can see the dilemma arising if our Angels appeared to us in human form. It would be helpful to accept our Angels that way, coming in to our lives at the time of need and looking as we do. The movie "Michael", starring John Travolta, gives us an interesting concept of the way an Angels could appear to us. We have no idea how God will have his or her subjects appear to us on Earth.

It would be nice if we could peek into God's great book of plans for us - and the world we live in. There are times when, without thinking about Angels, I receive glimpses of their presence above me as if they are saying, "Here we are... What do you need today?" Offering their support and love to me as I ponder over some decisions I'm about to make. This is how they come to us unexpectedly and without warning.

Many people can feel or sense their presence and perhaps even see them near. Their input to each of us is wonderful, and can add new ideas and direction to our lives if we "*just*" listen, but that is one problem we often have doing. There is no question our Angels come with unconditional love for us. They prove this by just making the trip back to this world, a world of problems and all forms of distractions that hold us back. It is not an easy trip to make for either Spirit or Angel, for our world, in comparison to theirs, is quite bleak and without true beauty.

Angels will never force their will upon us, but instead attempt to help us on the path we choose to follow, and we need listen to them.

My guides have told me each of us has, already imprinted upon our souls, the directions that we will follow through life. It is a blueprint that is drawn in the world of spirit and must be followed to the "t" for us to learn the things we came back for.

If we deviate, as at times we do, our Angel helpers will do everything they can to get us back on track. They will not ask you to jump into the ocean unless they know you can swim, or to do something else you are not ready for. So the path we must follow is one that is already set for us, and it is up to us to stay on course.

In a way, it seems as though we are just puppets on a string, but we are not. We come back to learn and to grow, or to pick up where we left off, with the hope we won't have to do it again.

In some of the readings that I've done, I have seen Angels around the people attempting to give them messages they need, with the hope the Medium will relay it back to them

.

Now what do Angels look like? This is one of the questions I asked my Spirit Guides and, instead of giving me the answer they allow me to see the Angels more clearly. Some of the Angels are quite tall in appearance and others are small, almost like miniature dolls. Some come in as male others females. Most are quite beautiful, some in white and others dressed differently. I have even seen a homely angel. The number of Angels around a person varies at times; there could be one to several at one time. There are times when I don't see any at all with the person I am reading for. This doesn't mean the person is without an angel; it just means I am not seeing one around them at the moment. It's that simple.

Most of the people I know tell me they know their Angel force is with them at all times, and they depend upon them to give guidance.

There are times you will receive ideas or thoughts and say, "Where did this come from?" I am sure this is from your Angel or Angels prompting you to at least listen to what they are telling you, or to just do something you have put off, as we all tend to do. These messages are given with love and support to you at the time of need. There are many times when these helpers have stepped in to warn us of impeding dangers that may lie just around the corner. When you stop and think about it, you may have had such an experience when you were on your way somewhere, and in an instant made a sudden change from the path you were on to a new direction. Thus avoiding an accident or perhaps just meeting a person you haven't seen for years.

There are many stories of people who had the intent of going to one store, but abruptly changed their direction. They just "wound up" going to some other store and finding someone there who they needed to talk to. Other people have called upon their Angels to help them get a parking place in a crowded lot, and just as they started into the parking lot, a car pulled out, leaving the space that was needed.

One of my guides told me the other day the Earth is in need of help, and in the next few years there will be a large number of Angels coming to the Earth to help in the balancing of the planet itself. In fact, there are a few already here who will be starting the process. If we take a good look at the world today, one would think that help is needed now, not later. However, the time is not right for the process to begin. But it will start soon.

As we have seen, people are becoming more conscious of the world in which we live. Our awareness could mean these Angel helpers are nearer than we think. Perhaps we on the Earth are in some way preparing for this new event to happen.

This does not mean the world will be destroyed. Rather, it means that the world will have to make some changes to survive. Today there are more healing groups and people who are interested in learning more about the processes of the healing arts. These healing groups will spread out and form larger groups for the benefit of the world. If we are willing to work with our angel helpers, the world will survive. If not, our future is much less certain. This is up to each of us. This is our Earth, and we have the responsibility to take care of it.

"SOUL TALK"

One bright sunny day, I was in my little boat paddling from one side of the pond to the other in a state of meditation. One of my guides mentioned to me that I could talk to my own soul. My first reaction was "Right", and that someone from the other side was joking with me. Then it came to me that I was talking to my own soul and that it sounded as if I was talking to myself. I have since found that "why not"? This is the true self, so it would stand to reason that it would sound like the way we talk.

J: Marion, when you mention about our soul talking to us, what do you mean?

M: This is a good question and the answer is: each soul does talk to you if you request it to do so.

J: What do we say, "Speak"?

M: No, not at all. You just ask to have your soul to communicate with you as you would another person.

J: How will we know it is the soul, and not just our minds doing the talking?

M: This is where you must truly believe in what you people call "Faith".

J: When I communicate with my soul, it sounds like me doing the talking.

M: Well sure. But who are you, but the soul? So it would sound just like you talking to some one else.

J: I am sure that would be hard for some to believe in.

M: Yes, it is hard to believe in, however that is the way it is.

When you think about it, the one who would know the most about you would be you. The soul is with you all the time and came with you as you made the choice to come back to the Earth plane. Each of us can talk to our own soul and learn so much about ourselves – perhaps in a new way.

In order to understand the concept of talking to the soul, we have to understand what the soul is and what its function is. First of all I am not an expert on the subject, and I don't think anyone really is. I can, however, relate the information that has been given to me by my Spirit Guides, both Brother Francis (a monk who lived in the 19th century), and Gladys, whom I knew here on the Earth. Since her passing she has been my true guide in all my readings. This information has been coming from them each day, and they have been adding to it as time goes on.

Our understanding of the other world, and what goes on within it, is quite interesting, and we can learn a great deal as we peer inside. The other side is a fascinating system of organization that has been established by something or someone who has great amounts of knowledge and the wisdom needed to put it all together. It is doubtful we will ever understand the whole, or at least not until we go back there.

In most religions, little is known about the soul except from the standpoint of religious application, and the attempt to save it from the snares of the devil. The salivation of the soul is the theme that has been the foundation of religions for thousands of years, and has been written in our minds since we were children. It remains a central part of our thinking to this day. People have been struggling with this concept for so long that the churches are now in the process of trying to deal with it on a different level I think that this is desperately needed in order to help their flock understand that our souls do not need "saving", and neither do we as children of God.

According to both my Spirit Guides, the soul is the aura field that surrounds each of our bodies with its streams of light, taking on different shapes. This soul, or aura, can extend many feet from the body at certain times, depending upon your rate of vibration (we are all sources of energy) and your state of being at the time. For example, if you feel good about yourself and everything is going well in your life, the aura will reflect this by extending out from the body with a glow of brightness radiating from it like the glow of the afternoon sun. If you are down on something, no matter how small it may be, the aura wilt also reflect that mood, and can perhaps be seen as a diminished brightness, like a pale a reflection of light from a distance.

Our soul will change depending on our moods and reactions to life. Our soul also reacts to the way we feel and think in a lot of different ways. Since our soul and aura responds similarly, I believe that the soul and the aura are one and the same. This statement will, I am sure, cause some who have studied the Auric field over the years, to disagree.

The aura is an energy field, and some have a color base to them as the field radiates from the body. This aura or energy field is emitted by just about everything that we know of, including both seen and unseen objects. Kirlian photography was used in an experiment in which a leaf was bisected and photographed using a special camera designed to capture the energy, or aura. When developed, the films showed the energy, or aura, of each of the two halves attempting to reach out to the other.

Could this be the soul? And then there was the picture of the human finger that was also photographed by this same camera showing the emanation of the lights that came from it. Could this be an extension of the soul?

As my guides have informed to me, the soul has many parts to it, and can do a great deal more than we ever thought. We could be talking about a multi-dimensional soul that has many functions, including the ability to travel at will.

One day as I was walking, Brother Francis, one of my guides, was again with me as he usually is, giving me information about the soul and other things that I should know about. He mentioned that the soul extends a lot farther than we had thought, some times great distances from the physical body. Brother Francis pointed out a person about thirty feet from where we were, and said that my soul could touch his at that distance and even beyond. That was news to me, because I have always thought that the aura, or in this case the soul, could not reach that far and, as he mentioned, in all directions. It shows that we still have little knowledge of everything that we think we do, and there is so much more to learn.

The soul is the storehouse for all information, including the so-called book of records, or the Akashic records, that we have been hearing about over the years. This record of all our past, present and perhaps future, is contained in this record that has been a mystery for so long. We as humans tend to look outside ourselves for what is right within each of us. This means that all we have done or accomplished in our lives are right here within us. On some occasions, such as when we are sleeping or perhaps in a very light trance state, some of us may tap in to our souls and review our life experiences, including past lives. Remember that these experiences are all part of us – nothing is wasted in the spirit world. If all this is true (and I have no doubts that it is), then what a wonderful machine each one of us really is, and how truly close we are to God.

If our souls are the true "us" and are the extensions of us, then it would be conceivable to communicate with that part of us. This sounds somewhat strange, however when you think about it, who else knows more about you than the "one" you came here with, your soul? Remember that we did not come to the Earth alone, and we have had not only our souls, but also guides to support us in our understanding of Earth life - then and now. I believe that the soul has imprinted in it every detail of our next "landing" here on this plane. It does all that so it can keep us on the right track for soul growth.

Looking at it in a different light, the soul is a guide that we never call upon though it is much closer to us than even our spirit guides and helpers. One of the reasons is the fact that in order for "The Spirit Guides" to reach us, they must travel through a lighter field of vibration to a denser one here on Earth, whereas the soul is already here in the material field with us.

This does not mean that we should disregard our Spirit Guides and Helpers. We need our souls, guides and helpers working with us as a team. Like any working team, trying to do things all "on your own" does not work.

Communication with one's soul is not out of the question, and one frequently asked question that comes up is, "how does one communicate with the soul?" Here is what I recommend as a reply: find a nice, quiet place in your home where there is no noise or disturbances of any kind. Sit in a nice comfortable chair and close your eyes. Take three deep breaths. Then, just ask for your soul to talk to you.

You may want to start off with a question like, "Am I going to be all right in my life", whatever question you ask, you will receive an answer.

Remember, this will take practice and therefore a little time to accomplish. It doesn't come overnight, so just be patient.

You might wonder what the soul sounds like. It does not have a loud beep voice, as if you were listening to Moses as played by Charlton Hesston. That is not the way you talk, is it? I don't think so. The soul is you and the voice is you, but the difference is that it will tell you what you never knew.

The way the soul will come in is a lot different than you might expect. The way you communicate is the way your soul talks to you. Remember, your soul is the extension of you. In fact, it is the true you. We are souls enclosed in a physical body, not the other way around. The way to activate the soul for conversation is to simply ask the soul to communicate with you. That sounds a little silly and too easy, but why not? You and your soul are one, so why not just ask!

As my guides have mentioned many times, we humans make life too hard for ourselves, and that is why we miss so much when working with spirit. On the Earth side, we always look for facts to back up all statements, and if we cannot get these facts then the understanding is incorrect and is lost. There are some things that cannot now, and perhaps never, be explained - but we must learn to accept what is given to us from the world of spirit.

We have seen the soul in the Auric form, but it does not have the color that we seem to think is there in the field. The color is our perception, and that is all. I would like to mention that I also see the aura colors around objects, and can interpret meanings of the Auric colors thanks to information from my guides. Are the colors really there? Possibly not, but we are so used to seeing colors, that spirit has provided the idea and perception of colors.

When we see paintings that were created in the early history of Christianity, of the Christ child and his mother Mary (along with all the saints), we note the halo, or aura, that surrounds the head or whole body of the persons depicted. Could this be the soul of the individual that is depicted on the canvas? More than likely it is the soul that we are seeing through the eyes of the gifted artist, and, if that is true, then we know what the soul looks like, and that it has some form of substance and weight.

If my guides are right, and I have no reason to believe that they are not, the soul has a great many facets and functions, which we have overlooked for many years. As I mentioned earlier in this Chapter, the soul has the ability to communicate with us, and holds a great amount of information that has been part of us as long as we have existed. Talking to the soul is one thing we have not only forgotten to do, but we think that it is impossible. Yet what I have told you is that it is one of the important reasons that were given to each of us.

The soul is mufti-dimensional in nature, which means that it can be in as many places at a time as it elects, and in some cases will do just that. At night while asleep, we do leave the physical body, and go to the other plane and come back in the morning. In a relaxed state of consciousness we can do the same thing while awake. This is one of the reasons my guides have advised me to use centering... in which you still the mind and become in tune with yourself. Some call it "the breath", and I am sure there are other names one could put on it. The idea is to find a nice quiet place, and take three deep breaths and become in tune with yourself. In this state you can also be in tune with your soul, talk with it and start receiving a wealth of information.

The interesting information my guides have told me is that the so-called heaven is a state of consciousness in which the person increases his or her rate of vibrations. The concept of hell is a product of the lower rate of vibration that a person is in at the time.

There is also a blending of souls, and that can occur at any time. If we could rise high enough to see all the souls, they would, from a distance, look like busy streetlights in the night sky. Each soul knows, and unites with others from their past. The aura that we see is the soul as it appears from the other side, or what we call the world of spirit. Your soul will keep away the spirits that should not be within your field of influences, which means that the soul acts as a "guard at the gate" for you. Each person has a soul. Even God has a soul. The waters, trees and everything around us have a soul. There are many facets to the soul, many ways it reaches out to us, and many ways

"GOING DOWN"

As I said before; "Its a boy! Eight pounds and twenty-one feet long." That's what I said when I called my mother-in-law with the news that our first child, John, was born. Her first comment was: "what do you have there" I had to compose myself and recalculate, and said, "You're right, it's a little boy, not a whale!" As you might expect, the next two were announced with a little more accuracy!

When a child is born, it's the *greatest!* When we have the time to think about it, most of us will stop and reflect upon life and its mysteries. We hope that our child will somehow follow in our footsteps as we followed our parents. That is not always true, as many of us have discovered.

The mother goes through a great deal in the nine months of pregnancy, but upon arrival of the child, all is somehow forgiven. There is a glow that seems to emanate in the room, and it is one of joy and love, and is also in the heart of the mother as she watches her baby look up at them with the smile of success.

As time passes, the child takes on its own characteristics, and as time continues, the child becomes its own person, and eventuality matures into adulthood. It all seems so natural, until we realize what happens behind the scenes of the master plan on the other side of life, and the many things that the child has to go through in order to get to that place.

One day I was communicating with Brother Frances. He is one of my guides who has been with me on the other side since before my birth, and has been with me for all the time of my Earth - bound existence. He will stay with me until it is time for me to go back home to the world of spirit. Each of us has such a guide who stays with us through our journey here and back. He explained to me what we go through before birth and the support that is given from others who have been through the process of returning to the Earth plane. This process is long, well planned and comes with a great deal of support from many that come in to help.

Sometimes there is a tremendous amount of questioning about our journeys. But the major factor is that we do not come alone, or without some knowledge of where we are going.

When we travel back to this plane, we do so with our guide, and the blessings of the council that is the support body for all who want to make the journey back to Earth, just as we have while we are here on Earth.

Some of the choices we make before we arrive on the Earth include such issues as why we want to come in the first place, and what are we to do once we arrive. Let me describe a case without using names or the place where the reading took place. This will demonstrate the example of early choices that are made even before we arrive here.

A client came for a reading and in my message I explained that my guide saw a baby around her, which usually means that she miscarriage at some point in her life. Gladys also told her that it was not her fault for loosing the child. My guide also mentioned the sex of the child, and the mother had a feeling that Gladys was right. She thanked me for confirming something that she has felt over the years.

It gives me a good feeling to know that I, with the aid of my guide, can help a person who is in need. This reading not only gave comfort to the mother, helping her to cope a little better with the loss, and taking the weight off her shoulders as she realized that her child was doing fine in her home on the other side.

In the readings I do, I don't remember what spirit has said to the one who I have read for at the time, even if it was just the other day. That's the way I like it. I have found it is the best way, allowing me to live in the world that I am currently in, without becoming a storehouse for all that information.

I was talking to a woman the other day that is a psychic, and she was telling me that she was fearful of the impressions she was feeling with people. She mentioned that she read for a young woman who just came on staff, and she automatically tuned into her without the young woman's knowledge and became drained because of it. She mentioned that sometimes it could be so easy for her, that she doesn't know how to turn it off when she needs to.

She and I spent some time talking about how not to tune in to a person unless asked to do so, because it is like violating the person's privacy.

I told her that in my estimation, it was not only a violation of ones rights, but it is not good for the Medium to take on the entire emotional load. She understood what I was saying and asked me how to stop doing this.

I don't remember the readings that I do, nor do I want to. I don't want old information to interfere with the current reading I am doing. So when my guide gives me some or all of the past readings that I have done for someone, I have to use it only with the intent of helping others to understand the messages that are being given, or to let them know it does work.

As Mediums, we do out best to help those that come for the reading with their daily lives, and to help those who are about to make the transition to the other side.

Because of these and other experiences that have I have encountered involving the spirit world, I asked my guide, Brother Francis, on one bright and cloudless day, "What happens in the world of spirit prior to the entity coming to the Earth?"

I will give you this information as it came from him, as he outlined it in his usual quiet way:

"In the world of spirit there is a rather long process that is performed before we make the journey to Earth and encounter the new experiences that we will go through while here." It is preparation for the ups and downs this world has to offer. As I mentioned before, we have choices here as well as over there in the spirit side of life. To make these choices, we have to depend on our guides and helpers for advice. It is these choices, such as whether we can effect to travel back to the Earth (or to other worlds) that we have to deal with. We came back here because our souls, the true essence of ourselves, wanted to head back to this world of matter in order to accomplish what we need to learn and perhaps what we missed the first time.

I have some feelings about the concept of karma, and the debit and credit system it offers. It teaches that we come back to make amends for what we did or did not do. I personally have doubts about that belief system.

I believe one of the intents of returning is to learn something new about ourselves that will help us become more aware of the importance of what we are all about, along with our place in the universe, and most of all to learn more about God and the creators great plan. Whatever the purpose, back we come ready to experience the material world again, but hopefully from a different perspective. After we've arrived, we sometimes have what we call flashbacks of where we just came from, including the people we left behind.

Some of us will have stronger flashbacks of former lives than others. It can make us stop and think that perhaps we are "Losing it ". But in most cases, we are having a real recall of not only you're past lives, but also of the place we left before coming here.

Before we enter the Earth plane, we meet our guide who will become a large part of our travel to the Earth, and also go to a council of elders, ones who will help us in our descent to Earth, They also help us go over what we must know in order to handle the difficulties that we all have to encounter.

From what I have been told by Brother Francis, the members of the council will try to talk us out of coming back because of the denseness of the Earth itself and the problems that we will face, but because we want to learn more, and perhaps teach others what we feel, we elect to make the trip back.

It is of interest to know that we make the trip back with great love and understanding. We must have these traits within us before we come back. While on the other side, we make the preparation for our journey here like an airplane pilot plots the course to get to one place as safely as possible. The council will help us with all the material we need, and assign us a guide, to make the trip as smooth as possible. The distance may not be far to travel, but the risk could be great. Remember, we will be traveling to a much denser world than the one we are leaving, and because of the problems we'll have here, we must make the right decision to come back.

Let me explain where the world of spirit is, in relation to our world. The spirit world is very close to the Earth. It is only separated from the other side by the rate of vibration. I tell my students that we could be walking in the home of one who is in spirit and not even know it. That is how close the spirit world is to ours.

There are other planes of existence that have a higher rate of vibration in which spirit could go. Perhaps that is what Jesus meant when he said, "In my Father's house there are many Mansions"

The time you and your guide spend with the council, and when you make the start to Earth is not clear, as our time is quite different than theirs. Brother Francis has said, that it is not that long, but we here on the Earth measure time a lot differently than they do, so it may appear to us a long time.

I tried to get Brother Francis to change their time so our time will be the same as theirs, which would be nice, but it didn't happen!

Whatever the period of time that goes by, before you and your guide (or guides) start your decent to the Earth, you will fully be aware of the Earth and all that you need to know. As you come here, new experiences will clutter your mind and you will close your mind to the past lives and experiences you left. I believe that for a while, you still experience some flashes of the world you left, and you see your Spirit Guide with you for some time until society takes over.

Stop and think, when was the last time you peeked into your child's room, where he or she was playing, and saw that child talking or playing with some unseen person in the room? Could this be their Spirit Guide who came with them? In most cases it is, and unless we are aware, we either think that our child has a vivid imagination, or perhaps the child is not well.

Brother Francis told me that he has my book of effects; this is a book like the Akashic Records, a book that was constructed while we were back in the world of spirit. It gives us the road map for the direction we are traveling on the Earth. If we stay on the course that is laid out for us we will accomplish a great deal of what we came here to achieve.

Each of us has such a book, and each of us must learn to follow the guidance we receive from our Spirit Guide. When I get down and feel that life is not on my side, my guide will impress upon me that I have deviated from the course that was written for me. I need to get back on track and forge on with the work that I came here to do, thinking more positively about myself, and as they say, "Go For It".

They have great advice - advice that I wish all of us would follow. Each of us must work with our guides and pay attention to what they tell us. I wont tell you that if you do, all is going to be great in your life, but by paying attention to what they tell you, it will become a great deal easier to go on, and that, in itself, is where we want to be.

The idea of having a book of effects, as it is called, sounds fatalistic in nature to me, except that each of us has free will and can make changes as we choose. That means we do not have to follow what they say - we can choose to "go it on our own" and do the best we can.

As for me, I will listen to my guide and do the utmost to stay on the course that was laid out for me. They do all this with love and the blessings of our creator, so why would I go against all that work?

I have read for many people who have been here more than once, and who are still doing their best to learn all that is needed to know about themselves and their creator.

There are souls that come back to meet what is called their "soul-mate ", and in most instances will follow the plan outlined in of the book of effects in order to do so. In the world of spirit there is a great deal of planning that takes place, and there are many who are involved in the process of going over with the candidate the facts that going back to the Earth will mean he or she has heavy responsibilities to deal with.

As you can tell, there is a lot of preparation before we venture here from start to finish for both our Spirit Guide and ourselves who is make the journey together

TESTIMONY

John Roger's extraordinary ability to communicate with several spirit guides on the other side is intriguing as he goes into areas of which one can only dream. In this unique work, through a series of conversations with his spirit guides, he examines the relationship between those who have passed over, our own souls, and the lessons we are here to learn. A misconception that most people have is that death is the end. Even though it may be the conclusion of one's own physical being, death is just the beginning of our soul's journey onward. For those of you looking for the why's to your questions, "The Medium Within" may just have the answers!.

Susan Mionske
Palm Bay, Florida

We all have questions about what happens to us when we depart the body we "rent" for our stay in this life. We hear about mediums, spirituality, guides and angels, and usually wind up with even more questions. It's refreshing to read a book which chronicles a spiritual minister's personal quest for answers to his questions and in so doing, helps us answer many of our own. Very interesting reading!

Dr. Stephen G. Rudin
Brockton, Ma

John's book is very enlightening and extremely easy to follow, especially for those of us who are novices in this subject. Excellent readings!

Mary Rohrer
Melbourne, Fl.